'This set of essays is a series of meditations on hatred, tenderness, grief, mourning, labour, resistance, social justice and the possibilities of meaning and solidarity, all viewed through the lens of some traumatic events that have convulsed India in recent years. It is an insightful, unusual guidebook that illuminates the path that we as a country and as a people took, to arrive at the dangerous place in which we are now.'

ARUNDHATI ROY

Author of *The God of Small Things*

'Powerful. Brahma Prakash's narrative, in beautiful prose, describes the barricades that India's women, men and children face on a daily basis. His spotlight shines on the societal curtailments, part and parcel of Hindu society, which have incrementally and maliciously permeated Indian politics. He shows us how the light in dark days is to be found in the resilience and inspiration of academics, activists, artists, Adivasis, and those imprisoned without bail or trial. I can't recommend Prakash's work of passion strongly enough. Be prepared to pause and contemplate his words.
Be prepared to get enraged.'

SANTOSH DASS

Co-author and co-editor, *Ambedkar in London*

'Leisure affords contemplation, but during a time of great
turmoil it is corporeality which teaches one philosophy.
What you can learn in a few hours being on the side of
barricades where the oppressed stand up to the mighty,
cannot be learnt spending years in a library. In this book,
Brahma Prakash recounts what authoritarianism feels
like in our bones. A book for the time which feels like an
aberration but when 'business as usual' revealed itself to
our collective naked eyes its grotesque,
revolting, suffocating truth.'

GHAZALA JAMIL
Professor, Jawaharlal Nehru University

'Lyrical, searing and powerful, *Body on the Barricades*
addresses political struggle as performance, making
visible protest as embodied, dramatized. The body
bearing its caste, gender, religious community identity,
is presented in the thick of battle against the coercive
power of the state, of dominant groups. Scholarly rigour
blends with the power of emotions that set this body,
these bodies, in motion — rage, grief, solidarity, love,
hatred. Brahma Prakash's book bears witness to one of
the darkest, but also most inspiring moments
in the history of India.'

NIVEDITA MENON
Professor, Jawaharlal Nehru University

'This book is an extraordinary examination of the politicking, grieving, protesting body. From choked breath to the taken 'knee' and flogged back, and from the curtailed tongues of poets to plastic extracted from the bellies of cows, it sweeps a broad arc across contemporary politics, all the while rooting for the flesh and blood and tears of human bodies.'

ANNIE ZAIDI

Author of *Prelude to a Riot*

'Brahma Prakash's *Body on the Barricades* is a searing cultural critique of the contemporary nation body. It is a commentary on the everyday life of love, labour, art and protest. It captures a moment when the nation's body is barricaded not just by its borders but by its segments: region, religion, caste, gender, and class. Authoritarian regime turns the Covid-19 pandemic into a site to practice segregation, division and suppression of the poor and the vulnerable. People can't speak, mourn, write, read, march, and not even breathe. The book is polemical, poetic, and sharply political. A must read to understand and contest the politics of hate and majoritarianism of our times.'

K. SATYANARAYANA

Professor, English and Foreign Languages University

BODY ON THE BARRICADES

BODY ON THE BARRICADES

Life, Art and Resistance
in Contemporary India

Brahma Prakash

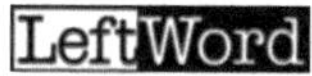

First published in May 2023
Reprinted July 2023, September 2023

LeftWord Books
2254/2A, Shadi Khampur
New Ranjit Nagar
New Delhi 110008
INDIA

LeftWord Books and Vaam Prakashan are imprints of
Naya Rasta Publishers Pvt. Ltd.

leftword.com

ISBN   978-93-92018-10-7 (paperback)
          978-93-92018-14-5 (e-book)

Digital print edition, July 2024

Contents

Prologue   11

1. **When We Can't Breathe**   25

   Living with Curtailment

2. **Words and Demagogues**   46

   What Demagogues Do With Words

3. **'Will You Hate Him, as You Hate Me'**   68

   Muslim Hating in the Bone of the Nation

4. **Dance of the Migrant Labourers**   92

   When Migrants Deviate from the Route

5. **The Trial of Art**   114

   Poets, Artists and the Authoritarian State

6. **March of the Mustard**   134

   Protest, Dissent, and the Curbing of Rights

7. **A Siege Against the Siege**   156

   The Larger Significance of the Una Strike

8. **A Show for the Dead**   182

   Death, Mourning, and Solidarity

Epilogue   201

Yet, Not Yet over

Acknowledgements   207

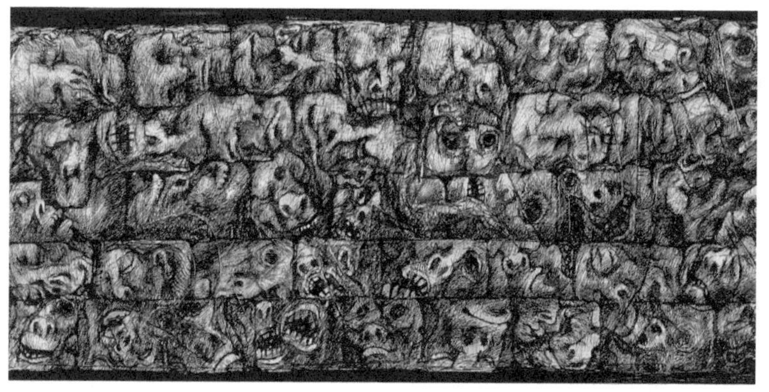

Prologue

> *This is precisely the time when artists go to work.*
> *There is no time for despair, no place for self-pity,*
> *no need for silence, no room for fear. We speak, we*
> *write, we do language. That is how civilizations*
> *heal.*

— Toni Morrison[1]

It was April 2021. A ghastly month for India. The second wave of the Covid-19 pandemic ravaged the nation like a tsunami, moving so fast that before people could grasp its reality, they were in its grip, yearning for life and gasping for breath.

While working on this book of essays, I, too, caught the virus. The moment came for me too. Breathlessness suddenly became raw and real for me. Like a live wire, it entered my nerves. With an oximeter attached to my fingers and a thermometer on my tongue, I too felt the urgency of life.

Moments turn into events when you start counting every breath. You count the heartbeat. You count your pulsating veins. You count blood vessels and bones. You become a vigilante of your own body. You never know when lungs and bones can turn white or black, when blood will turn into water, and disappear from the body like vapour. You keep checking if the skin is changing its colour. Devoured by the virus, you check that your eyes aren't turning black. You still see. You still think. You still register. You still resist.

---

[1] Toni Morrison, 'No Place for Self-Pity, No Room for Fear', *The Nation*, 23 March 2015.

Before I proceed and you preside, let me clarify that this is not a book on the pandemic. The references to the pandemic repeat, only to surface a symptomatic condition of the curtailment of life. The book is about a pandemic-like situation. The urgency of life and the barricading of freedom. The dilapidated socio-political and health condition that Naren Bedide stated, 'India is the pandemic.'[2] His insistence on the statement also shows how seriously are we taking these issues. The book is about earnest hope in the face of extreme curtailment.

In the urgency of life, the body takes all the attention. It takes all the forms; it takes all the shapes; it takes all the toll. You writhe like a fish out of water. You crawl like a worm, making all kinds of shapes. You move slowly, like a Japanese *butoh* dancer on a bed. You feel blockages you have never felt. You feel the openings you have never thought. You see the thoughts you have never seen. Out of fear of the virus, you check everything. You clean the broom and sanitize the sanitizer. You bathe the water before you take a bath. When fear enters our psyche, we become suspicious of everything. We suspect everyone.

The barbed wire used during Covid-19 in Delhi and Mumbai reminds us about the caste, race and ghettoised society. It reminds us of what B.R. Ambedkar said, 'It is a case of territorial segregation and of a *cordon sanitaire* putting the impure people inside a barbed wire into a sort of a cage.'[3] Fear, suspicion, rumour, invisible enemies, and zones connect the coronavirus to an extreme culture of authoritarianism. The 'identification, confinement, the drawing of boundaries and a strategy of exclusion have produced the reality of race in history.'[4]

---

[2] Naren Bedide, 'India is the Pandemic,' Goethe Institute, 14 October 2020. https://www.goethe.de/en/kul/ges/eu2/tlk/22008456.htmll

[3] B.R. Ambedkar, *Dr Babasaheb Ambedkar: Writings and Speeches* (henceforth *BAWS*) Vol. 7 (New Delhi: Dr Ambedkar Foundation, Reprinted 2014 [1987]), 266.

[4] Ranabir Samaddar, *A Pandemic and the Politics of Life* (New Delhi: Women Unlimited, 2021), 9.

As news of deaths and mayhem came, I, too, felt extreme despair. I, too, felt confined to my bed, in my body and space, the world turned into confinement. The body on the barricades became too real to be a metaphor. It was painful to see people dying of suffocation. It was painful to see how much you can concede. How much can you contain? How much can you squeeze? Full of indignity, you feel helpless and halved. Still, at the cusp of mourning and mayhem, you see new solidarities in the making. People were risking their lives and coming out on the streets to save lives. In the absence of government, they were creating a parallel system. That appeared like a new possibility, a new assembly.

What about the others? What about the sanitation workers who work in the sewers? There, the suffocation does not come as a surprise. The pandemic is a life they live every day, indignity is a general condition of living and being choked to death is the most common bulletin of dying. Breathlessness is a general condition of life. They already live in quarantine maps. When they are born, their birth is marked. When they walk, their bodies get marked. They carry marked bodies through life and death. Every day, they walk into quarantine zones.

Curtailed movements create choreographic patterns. They enter the bones and become part of muscle memory. Sometimes keeping bodies on the barricades, sometimes hiding behind the barricade, they learn to walk. Caste society has produced, perhaps, the most conscious act of walking, for women and outcastes. One must be aware of social status while walking. They not only define the social rules; they also govern the aesthetic rules.

The Indian aesthetic text, the *Natyashastra*, prescribes how the lower castes and women should walk. What should be the 'gaits' of lowly people: 'persons of inferior birth are to walk with eyes looking around, protecting their limbs from the contact of other people.'[5] The restrictions are embodied. Movements are marked

5 Bharata-Muni, *The Natyashastra*, translated by Manmohan Ghosh (Calcutta: The Asiatic Society, 1961), Vol. 1, Ch. XIII, 150.

in relation to social positions. They are marked on temple walls, instilled in schools, installed in institutions. They are in social codes, in the walks, gaits, and greets. They carry this internalized prescription in their eyes. *They will stare at you, but keep your eyes low*. The curtailment of movement has slowly cut the bone. They limp when they walk; they cripple when they move. They cannot stand properly. It breaks their backbones every day. They have been walking a curtailed walk. What you are seeing is not always sexy curves; it can be a curbed body in sexual codes like the Chinese foot-binding that produces lotus feet. While the woman cries in pain, lotuses spring from her every step for the connoisseurs. In the name of art and tradition, appreciation and objectification go together.

The pandemic brought with it a new condition of life for many. But for many others, the conditions were already like this. It was there, you're not interested in seeing it. You behaved like Gandhi's three monkeys who decided not to see, not to hear, and not to utter a word. At the height of the pandemic, Kishor, a sanitation worker, decided to get married. 'Are you mad? Postpone it', I asked with great concern. He smiled. He changed the topic. 'Sir ji! How do you people maintain the double mask?' he asked, seeing me in a double mask. I felt exposed. Good that he did not say, 'Sir, your mask is falling down.'

Perhaps, I was in a bad dream. I woke up to another world. The protestors of Shaheen Bagh were still out there. They're still building their assembly body by body. Sanitation workers participated in a strike again in Delhi for the right to life. They marched with the new slogan of Safai Karmchari Andolan, 'Stop Killing Us,' to reclaim their dignity, equality, and personhood. They marched against the inhuman practices of manual scavenging which remains banned in the law but open to practice.[6] Adivasis in central India led one

---

[6] Safai Karmchari Andolan (SKA) is an organization that is fighting to put an end to manual scavenging in India.

of the biggest marches against the barricading of their movements in the forests. The Kashmiris were carving out their alternative assembly in the protest marches.

Outside the legitimised assembly and parliament, protestors were creating alternative assemblies on the roads and streets, in the valley and forests. Resistance was not yet over. Humanity suffered immense loss, but it was not yet dead. Everything was not yet over. Amidst the pandemic, Kishor left for his marriage with *band, baja,* and *baraat.*[7] The young danced for the new love and renewed their commitment to life. They danced parallel to the dance of death that the virus directed. Can you stop them from falling in love? Can you ask them to go against life's urges? Can you stop them from merrymaking?

Cuckoos returned to the garden. A friend wrote that flowers bloomed again on her balcony. Others asked, 'Can we go for a drink again.' We wished again. We kissed again. We went for a walk again. We marched again. Life could not be bullied under any circumstances.

Body on the Barricades is a book of essays on the curtailment of life, art, and freedom in contemporary India. It is about a situation that stands at the edge. One stands at the margin. It also shows how politics and aesthetics are coming to a corporeal level, entering our psyche, playing out on our bodies and mind every day. We start thinking from the barricades in a situation of extreme vulnerability. It is the situation in which we enter the state of *non possumus: We can't return. We can't yield anymore.* It is the limit of concession after one can't surrender. But you can't stand motionless at the barricades. It is the limit but also the last base from where one can resist. It is the last site from which new politics and culture may emerge. We risk spaces. You are aware that if you move a step ahead, the authority may shoot you down. But two steps will bring life and freedom. Not doing anything will bring

---

[7] Celebratory wedding procession in India with music, song, and dance.

nothing. This fear of the end and the temptation for freedom keep changing the axioms of art and life.

Body on the Barricades is about thinking about life and freedom from the points of confinement. It is about the act of breathing from the point of breathlessness. It is the ultimate resolution of the body to cross the barbed wires. It is the situation in which we cannot breathe but we breathe. As the authoritarian regime pushes its boundaries, curtails our life and freedom, we have no option but to walk. The situation gives birth to a new politics, a new resistance, new resolution, a new realization. Breathing — a natural and unconscious act — becomes a conscious act. What was physiological becomes political. The right to breathe becomes a new assertion, name of a bare minimum that one asks for.

Breathlessness becomes a slogan and acquires a symbolic utterance in which one says, 'I can't breathe.' Let's not have any illusions of comparative analysis. The point is not to compare the meaning of 'I can't breathe' in the United States and India or between Black Lives and Dalit Lives. The point is to think through the symptomatic condition. It can be about the Blacks; it can be about Dalits; it can be about refugees; it can be about the poor and women. It can be about us. Philosopher Franco "Bifo" Berardi discussed this condition through the same evocation of 'I can't breathe' in the background of the racial murder of Eric Garner in 2014. He observes:

> In many ways, these words express the general sentiment of our times: physical and psychological breathlessness everywhere, in the megacities choked by pollution, in the precarious social condition of the majority of exploited workers, in the pervading fear of violence, war, and aggression.[8]

Nobody is saying that things were ideal before. Yet, whatever

---

[8] Franco "Bifo" Berandi, *Breathing: Chaos and Poetry* (South Pasadena: Semiotext(e), 2018), 15.

little has been achieved through long struggles, such as women's rights, rights of equality, and social justice, are under assault by conservative right-wing politics and the neoliberal regime. Egalitarian politics is on the back foot. The people who were asking for the distribution of lands are trying to defend their lands. This comes as a dangerous reversal. In the context of this background, this book of essays shows where we stand now and how much this regime has pushed us, how much more we can concede.

From the curtailment of the freedom of expression to the curtailment of fundamental rights, the Indian state has run riot. Under the leadership of Prime Minister Narendra Modi and the ruling Bhartiya Janata Party (BJP), it has laid siege to the body and democracy. It has led to a lockdown of almost all spheres of life. It is clamping down on dissent and protests. While this curtailment under neoliberalism is witnessed the world over, the Modi regime has worsened it. It is pushing the limits. It is fishing into the nets. It is testing our level of endurance. It has gone for the guts.

Curtailment can be of many things: body, words, rights, dissent, arts, expressions. Barricading can come in many forms: walls, ghettos, merits, aesthetics. Regressive values are not new to India. Who can access knowledge and who cannot? Who can walk across the board and who can't? In a caste society, bodies and spaces are already marked, so is the value of life. Borrowing from Judith Butler, you can always ask which life is more vulnerable. Which life you can easily dispose and which life you can't.[9]

Curtailment is a process that ferments slowly like culture itself. It invades body and space. It deceptively gives us a sense of security. It is encoded in the politics of neoliberalism that starts with austerity and security measures and ends with the thwarting of freedom and democratic rights. Resistance against curtailment becomes a matter of life and death.

It is a grave mistake to think that the rise of curtailment is

[9] Judith Butler, *Precarious Life: The Powers of Mourning and Violence* (London: Verso, 2004).

sudden. That it came with the rise of the rightwing politics of the Sangh and BJP's right-wing politics. The project of curtailment was already built into the fabric of Hindu society. With the nation, from the temple, the Brahminical body politic entered the parliament. It was moving slowly inwards into the heart of the nation's politics. The system's negligence and the state's culpability were not sudden. The rise of lynching mobs and the near-death of democracy were not so sudden. We are not talking about seven or ten years. We are talking about a condition that remains hidden in the Indian state's foundation itself. We are talking about the religion that has fouled the air. That has carried the spiral of hate.

A riot is not a spontaneous act. Genocide does not happen in one night. Hatred does not build in one day. It takes time to learn to hate. One has to learn and perform it constantly, like a religion and ritual. It has to be inflicted and tested frequently. Stigmatization and stereotypes have to be performed constantly to achieve a desired end. Branding is an endless temptation. Labelling is a reiterated act. The divide is not a boundary that one marks on the map; the divide becomes only real when it splits the heart.

This book of essays is about a curtailed condition of life that exists beyond the state of the coronavirus. The condition arises in a society of constraints and controls that tries to maintain hierarchies over bodies and spaces. It is about how the curtailment of life and freedom persists as the question of tyranny. It is about the bare politics of life that pushes us to the limits. In this work, I frequently draw from the pandemic because it made the bare politics more explicit. If curtailment is a premise of the study, the body on the barricades is the perspective and the site of study. The pandemic is just a pandora's box. I open this box from time to time to expose the problems of the authoritarian regime.

Barricade has a strange history. It is an object that people created on the streets to defend themselves against armies, but today it is turned against them. It has become an instrument in the hand of the police and armies to curtail movement.

One can read the symbol of the barricade differently as Eric Hazan did in *A History of the Barricade*.[10] In his reading, barricade emerges as a glorious emblem in the revolutionary struggle. But Hazan notes that the barricade gradually became marginal in the twentieth century: 'the physiognomy of cities has changed' and 'the armies assembled by the state to deal with civil war have been modernized'.[11] Extending his argument, we can say that the state appropriated the barricade as a strategy to stop people's movements. The deployment of the barricade is not only illegal and considered a crime, but social elites also see it as an object that disturbs movement and free circulation of capital. This suggests that the positioning of barricades becomes more sacrosanct than any specific meaning of barricade. It is all about who is placing the barricade, against whom, for what purpose. That means one is deploying barricades to suffocate others or to seek love and create zones of freedom.

The relationship between the body and the barricade is a layered one. We can think of different scenarios in which they come together. First scenario emerges in police and army action in which the body gets pushed by the barricades. In the second scenario, protestors erect barricades to push the authority. In the third scenario, barricade offers a security against the authority. In the fourth scenario, the body turns into barricades, a form of collective action and assembly. Here the body raises a barricade to exercise love and freedom where authority is not allowed.

In Utpal Dutt's famous play, *Barricade*, it appears as a potent weapon in the workers' hands. The *sutradhar* (narrator) says: 'But all the workmen on the planet know the word's meaning, because when you have to fight by blocking roads with dustbins, pipes and bricks, New York's Harlem and Kolkata's Khidirpur become one.'[12] But in the play, barricade is not only a physical object that workers deploy to obstruct and to strike; barricades also appear as agents and allegory of politics. The strength of the play lies in bringing all the agents of democracy to the barricades — to the point of confrontation. Barricades expose their 'neutral' position — they come out and encounter each other at the barricades. When the Nazis set books ablaze, apolitical Dr Mamlock renouncing his political position denounced the burning of books. The play situates the media, the polity, the judiciary, the intelligentsia, the citizenry in open encounter. The citizenry becomes the fences and the intelligentsia turn into the barricades. If the workers erect the barricades, intelligentsia hide behind them. In the aftermath of Naxalbari, when Indira Gandhi led Congress government was turning to authoritarianism, the play re-staged the Nazi takeover of Germany. Barricade is thought where thinking stops or one is persecuted for alternative thinking.

Body on the Barricades is about authoritarianism, its culture of curtailment, and the struggle against it. It is about the body resisting the barricades, breaking the barricades, crossing the barricades; in the absence of space, the body appearing on the barricades; or the body turning into barricade and creating space. When bodies assemble on the streets, they open time and space 'outside and against the established architecture and temporality of the regime' they are against.[13] Body on the barricades has its own dialectics. In the situation of extreme barricading, one has no option but to move. Against the barricading, movement is the utopia that gives us hope. But against the rampant movement and performance of capital, it is the barricade and the pause that create resistance.

There are no specific methodologies for these essays. The methodology of the heart carries the essays on their passionate turn. I am not a critic outside; I am part of it, sustaining the structure and feeling suffocated. There is duplicity behind my mask.

---

[13] Judith Butler, *Notes toward a Performative Theory of Assembly* (Cambridge, MA: Harvard University Press, 2015), 75.

Before the curtailment reached my home, I didn't see how others' lives were curtailed every day. The essays here are invitations for unveiling, unseeing, and seeing anew. An investigation in seeing, a bid to see why some lives are more grievable. From the points of curtailment, we are trying to see the possibility of solidarity. Solidarity from the sites of mourning, solidarity from the sense of grievability — where every life is grievable. Solidarity, not from the sense of freedom, but from the points of suffocation. Solidarity not from the graded positions but from a precarious position. This is important because solidarity from graded positions can only be caste solidarity. Thinking through the curtailment of life and freedom and resistance to it, I meditate on the cultural politics in contemporary India. Curtailment connects these essays. Sometimes it is the curtailment of the body; sometimes, it is the curtailment of words and movements. Amidst the curtailment, against the culture of silence, the essays also carry the indomitable spirit of art, life, and freedom.

Some sections of the essays have previously appeared as opinion pieces on various platforms, such as Café Dissensus, Hard News, Indian Cultural Forum, Karvaan India, *Outlook*, Scroll.in, and The Wire. The essays are often passionate and polemical. That is their style. I have attempted not to lose the nuances and sensibilities of the issues. I wrote them often in anger and frustration, and at moments when keeping quiet was harder. Like many writers, I believe epic tragedies and violence have to have an epic writing response; they cannot be captured merely by stating facts and information.

Chapters

The book has eight chapters. The first chapter, 'When We Can't Breathe', discusses the situation of breathlessness, which is a profoundly physiological and political situation. It discusses the situation's vulnerability and its immense mobilizing capacities in which every limb tries to act in defence of life. At that moment, what matters is not the lockdown but the deadlock — the impasse that irritates us and motivates us to participate in action. The chapter discusses this impasse between hope and hopelessness.

The second chapter, 'Words and Demagogues' discusses the curtailment of words by the culture of demagoguery. It argues that the curtailment of the word and the lynching of an individual are not separate acts. It shows how demagogues command through monologues and seize the very healing capacity of words.

Continuing the debate on the curtailment of words, the third chapter discusses how the new regime of control curbs minorities' lives and rights. Through my own family's stories and anecdotes, I tell the story of ghettoization and how hatred enters into bone.

The fourth essay brings forth the figures of migrant labourers and their plight in the light of the curtailment of bodies and movements. Migrant labourers neither belong to the villages nor the cities. They are called *pardesi* (outsiders) at home and *pardesi* outside. They are constantly on the move. During the Covid-19 pandemic, the authorities expected them to stay in one place or move in an assembly line. But, they drifted away from the designated routes. They undertook a walk that showed both the vulnerability and the potentiality of their movements.

The fifth chapter discusses the curbing of dissenting voices by the authorities. It discusses the tenuous relationship between art and the state. The chapter shows how the attack on poets and artists is an attack on indispensable human capacities. It is an assault on the bodies of sensibilities, the fundamental ideas of freedom, their rhythm, and words. It is an attack on the chord that echoes the unstuck word.

In the sixth chapter, I move to the curbing of protests with a focus on the farmers' protests in Delhi and its enduring spirit that led to the authoritarian regime's surrender. We learn a lesson that curtailment, unless opposed, never stops. It goes on to take over everything, from mourning to death. What happens when the right to protest is criminalized, when surveillance becomes the primary engagement of sovereign power? The media carries the same campaign with fear and hatred, with persistent demonization, with the harvest of shame.

Carrying the indomitable spirit of the farmers' protest, the next chapter discusses the unique gestures of protests that fall outside the accepted notion of protest, that is, nonviolent permissible protest within the limit or protest that happens within the space of appearances. In a biopolitical regime, *choreopolice* — movement decided by police — becomes the norm. Policing becomes the norm of protest itself (protest within 100 meters). The Dalits' outburst in the Una protest shows something else. It was about going outside the choreopoliced limit. It was about producing new gestures of politics itself.

The final essay discusses the banning of mourning and grieving in relation to the Hathras rape case in Uttar Pradesh and other sites. One can understand a situation where authorities fear protests and subversion. They are afraid of questions and criticisms. They are terrified of truth and dialogue. Why are they afraid of mourning and grieving? What do they find alarming in a wailing sound? What do they find dangerous in the last ritual? This essay connects us to mourning and its curtailment by an authoritarian regime in an oppressive social structure.

At the site of mourning and vulnerability, the Epilogue shows the possibilities of resistance and the fundamentals of life and art that cannot be curtailed under any circumstances.

language is indissociable...

1. When We Can't Breathe

Living with Curtailment

> *I believe in Liberty for all; the space to stretch their arms and their souls; the right to breathe and the right to vote, the freedom to choose their friends, enjoy the sunshine and ride on the railroads, uncursed by colour; thinking, dreaming, working as they will in a kingdom of God and love.*
>
> — W.E.B. Du Bois [1]

What would you do if you felt choked? You would try to breathe for life. When you feel clogged, you try to cough out. When you feel claustrophobic, you try to come out. If you are in a relationship that breaks you, you feel the need to break up. If you are in a village or in a city that blocks your way, you plan to run away. If you are in a culture or religion that gags your freedom, you seek escape from it. If you are in a nation that cannot provide a sense of belonging, you would ask the same question as B.R. Ambedkar or a refugee would ask: Where is my nation? Do I belong here? Can I breathe? Can I move without restrictions, without barricades? When air chokes and birds fall like a cloud of black smoke from a sky beaten black and blue by the rising city smoke, the chirping birds weep and ask in the tearful tune: 'where is my air?', 'where is my sky? We ultimately belong to air, to freedom!

The logic is simple. Breathing is elemental. Freedom is fundamental. Air is about existence. It is an elemental condition of

[1] W.E.B. Du Bois, *Darkwater: Voices from Within the Veil* (New York: Dover Publication, 1999), 2.

our life that cannot be compromised. The status of our rights and freedom depends on whether we have the right to breathe freely or not, whether we have the right to move freely or not. Breathing not only carries the fundamental act of life but also symbolizes the essential measure of rights and life of the mind. Body on the barricades indicates that bodies are positioned in an extreme situation teetering on the edge of hope and hopelessness. It is looming at large between life and death, moving across freedom and curtailment.

Breathlessness immediately brings us to the state of suffering with Covid-19. But it is a condition that exists beyond the disease. Murdered by the United States's racist ideology, George Floyd's cry in May 2020, 'I can't breathe', arose against the general dehumanized condition of life. Though breathlessness became paramount during the pandemic, it applies to many situations in which one feels suffocated — a state in which one feels out of breath, nearing death, losing hope but keeping alive like prey in the jaws of a predator. It is like a dying patient waiting for an ambulance as the last hope. It is like migrants walking on the rail tracks to reach home. Like minorities caught amidst a mob, hoping that the nation's conscience will arise from the crowd.

Yes, I feel I cannot breathe; therefore, I write. Whenever I feel suffocated, I write. Sometimes I write to write, sometimes I write to breathe. What I am feeling is not unusual. Many of us feel the same after seeing the sickening conditions around us: while reading the news, hearing lies, seeing mobs going mad in the streets, lynching bodies and words. We feel the same when we see ideals getting robbed. You feel suffocated when you see mobs enjoying violence, procuring power from vulnerability. You feel hopeless when you see the perpetrators of the crime obtaining political impunity to become the new generation of leaders in a nation claiming to be the *Vishwaguru* (global leader).

You feel suffocated when you see that hatred has reached your home. It walks with you as your friend, as a family member. You feel disheartened when you know they are building monuments of hate in the name of religion. You feel anxious when you see the virus moving in your workspace. It is dancing on your keyboards and screens — and jumbling words that you are terrified to see. Words are getting automated and anytime the virus can move against your body.

I take the risk to assume that at least some of us are feeling suffocated by the situation shaping Indian society. We are feeling barricaded, chained in our bodies and spaces. I am looking for words and phrases to describe the times we are living through. For me, no other words match the potential and vulnerability of 'I can't breathe'. I am looking for a figurative image that can capture this situation in body and action. The image I see is that of the body on the barricades.

'We'll Gather like Bees

In the simplest sense, 'we' is I and you. It is I and you, and you and you and you and you. We is the idea of coming together, in body and words, in alliances of bodies, in promised words that form a collective. But 'we' is the problem here. Perhaps it is the most fundamental problem of politics. It moves between the possibility and impossibility of marching together. It presents the challenge of coming together.

They say a collective is impossible. It's all fractures. It's all fragments. It's all false. It's a futile exercise. And thus, it's impossible to build solidarity. But that's the challenge. Of course, there is no easy way out. One has to be suspicious of 'we' when one speaks on your behalf. But 'we' also reminds us of our shared humanity, our commonality, our deep emotions that connect our emotional universe despite all the fractures and holes. Writer and activist bell hooks tells us, '[f]or across all differences of race, gender, class, sexuality, religion was a shared realm of emotional feeling'.[2] She

---

[2] bell hooks, *Yearning: Race, Gender, and Cultural Politics* (New York and London: Routledge, 2015), 16.

says our yearning for peace and justice might serve as a uniting force. She adds that the longing of our hearts is tied to the quest for freedom. 'A yearning for principled resistance and struggle can change our desperate plight', writes Cornel West in her endorsement. Thus, we have to come together. Collective is not a privilege, it is an urge. It is a necessity we cannot escape even if we differ radically. We need to find solidarity from the questions Toni Morrison asked: 'How people cry, how do they sleep, the sound of silence, rhythm of the body, color of the dawn, qualm of the dusk, failure of the movement, faith in the eyes, the conviction of the rebels, keep creating the sense of belonging, of possibility of the new world.'[3]

The shared space and feeling of breathlessness and yearning can offer 'the possibility of common ground where all these differences might meet and engage one another'.[4] In the loss of ideas and enthusiasm, the 'we' becomes our last hope, a witness of our last struggle. It is the principled position in which one asks for solidarity. It is in the positive feeling in which Ambedkar asks for *maitri* (fraternity). Fraternity here is not a feeling of brotherhood but feeling of fellowship — the term for collective caring that cuts across gender, caste, and race. Solidarity and fraternity are carried through cooperation, collective action, and mutual aid. Collective is not frozen like ice. It flows like water. Solidarity is not solid like a rock. It is a melting ground of bodies and ideologies. It is not an iron hook from which everyone has to be hanged, it is the gallows that bring bodies together beyond the boundaries for resistance. It is the name of the assembly, alliances and association.

What is fraternity? Ambedkar said that it is about the 'we-feeling' that brings us together. What casteist and racist ideologies kill is the very potential and principle of the 'we' feeling — the feeling

---

³ Toni Morrison, *Mouth Full of Blood: Essays, Speeches, Meditations* (London: Vintage, 2020), 21.
⁴ bell hooks, *Yearning*, 18.

of concern.[5] We become the common ground for the politics, for the change. 'We' brings 'I' and 'you' for a dialogue for change, in the march of struggle. 'We' is the agent of transformation. We have to change the 'we', so we can come together, we can march together for shared hope, for the shared future.

'We' is not based on a sense of privileges and valourization but a sense of vulnerability and longing. It carries the indefinability of plurality that cannot be named. If the sovereign power uses the idea of the 'we', so do poets, writers, and victims, such as in the case of the Black Lives Matter (BLM) protests. I use 'we' in the sense of I becoming you in love, in separation, in differences, and in a shared sense of vulnerability. It is like being together while apart. It is like a shaman embodying hills and forests and presenting a case of ecological destruction against humans. This can only become possible if we come to the extreme conditions of humanitarian thinking. 'We' gather when we think from the points of barricades, from zones of confinement, from what the philosopher Judith Butler would term as the moments of mourning and grievability.[6] We gather like bees around the flowers of life for their fragrance, fertilization, diversification, and the values that carry our life and struggle.

Yes, I feel like I cannot breathe. I am not George Floyd. My situation is not that of Elijah McClain, Eric Garner, Manuel Ellis, the Black men killed by the White ideology of the United States, or the Dalits and Muslims lynched by the Brahminical body politic of the Indian state. I am also not the unnamed others who breathed their last, pleading, 'I can't breathe'. I come from a low caste, but my situation is not that of the outcastes of Indian caste society whose whispers slowly sink into a sewer, and their trembling bodies do not find articulable words. Or even if they utter those words, they

---

[5] C.D. Naik, *Thoughts and Philosophy of Dr BR Ambedkar* (New Delhi: New Sarup & Sons, 2003), 2.

[6] Judith Butler, *The Force of Nonviolence: An Ethico-political Bind* (London: Verso, 2021).

go unheard, for who has heard their cries? Their unheard cries fail to find speech. Their broken bodies fail to assemble to make their appearance in a public protest. They die in a sewer without saying, 'I can't breathe'. But who has heard them? The tremor is there. But what is to be done when the collective conscience is dead? We need to find the answer to 'when we can't breathe'.

People from various sections of society have expressed their frustrations in the language of 'I can't breathe'. Carnatic musician and writer T.M. Krishna evokes the same when he says that a darkness suffocates him. He asks and answers. He feels the suffocation:

> Can darkness suffocate? It can block your sight. But can it stop you from breathing? Believe me, it can. The violence in thought, word and action around me, every day, every moment and in endless supply, is choking me. Like if my head was trapped in a plastic carry bag. A bag carrying messages — of hate.[7]

While there is no denial of the underlying differences and fractures, 'We can't breathe' still hints at a collective vulnerability. If the slogan captures George Floyd's murder, it can also capture the shortness of breath that suffocates Indian sanitation workers to death. It symbolizes the suffocating lives of women in the household. It also brings our attention to the ritualized spheres of social life or the communalized spheres of political life. It indirectly tells us: 'let's get out, I can't breathe', hinting towards a collective care and responsibility.

'We can't breathe' symbolizes the state of the prison we are in. But then, in the case of this prison, there is more equality. One is not talking about the communities that fill the prisons in India or

---

7 T.M. Krishna, 'Thought Controllers Are Making Us Hate Our Democratic, Plural Past'. Scroll.in, 18 February 2021, https://scroll.in/article/987260/tm-krishna-thought-controllers-are-making-us-hate-our-democratic-plural-past

the United States — Adivasis, Muslims or Blacks. One is talking about prison in an *ideal sense*. Then there is more equality in prison as the space of control reduces all the necessities to a bare minimum. In this case, Gandhi and Father Stan Swamy find prison life to be a great leveller. The precarity brings them to the most humanitarian level. Swamy writes:

> Inside the daunting prison gates
> All belongings were taken away
> But for the bare essentials
> 'You' comes first
> 'I' comes after
> 'We' is the air one breathes.[8]

As fragments, fragrance, the air and potential, we locate ourselves in this moment. Breathing is a fundamental condition of sharing; therefore, 'I can't breathe' is not a problem of I and you but of 'we'. We are the bodies on the barricades in all possible positions. One is spreading like a spider; others have enclosed themselves as snails. Sitting outside of it, others are yet planning to cross it.

The barricading that we are witnessing is not entirely new. Suffocation has not come with Covid-19. Lynching is not a new play that has come with a new regime. It has been in the power domain for a long time. We know that it is political. It is societal. It is suicidal. It has been coming for successive generations as part of the ritualized power and patriarchy. Hindi poet Ramashankar 'Vidrohi' finds its root in the old myth,

> The first case of lynching of a woman in history
> Was conducted by a son at the behest of his father
> Jamadagni asked his son Parshuram

---

[8] Stan Swamy, 'Prison life, a great leveller: Stan Swamy shares a poem from jail', 23 December 2020. https://sabrangindia.in/article/prison-life-great-leveller-stan-swamy-shares-poem-jail

That I ask you to kill your mother
And Parshuram killed his mother [9]

In the myth that becomes a model of the Brahminical body politic, Parshuram killed his mother by severing her head with an axe to set an example that a woman has no right to express her desire. And curtailment continued in the name of religion, in the name of culture, in the name of nation, honour and tradition.

Some of us were in denial of this curtailment because it had not come to us. Some of you are still in denial because of your privileges. You are also in denial because you are a beneficiary of this violent culture. But it was there in the Dalits' *basti*s (settlements), in the Adivasis' Bastar, and in Kashmir's valleys, it was marching on the hills of the Northeast regions. The notification was always there for the de-notified communities considered as born criminals. Curtailment was there in the lives of the groups and communities where your superior sense of the social always regarded them as anti-social. It was there for women; it was in every household. When refugees were out of homes, when nation-states were piling their bodies into boats, we were enjoying the citizens' impunity. We didn't notice it because it did not affect us. But for the others, it had become their normal. Thus, when we cry, nobody comes to console us. You feel fascism when it comes to you, but you were in denial when they were facing the indignity in everyday life. Their right to human existence was denied. Why do you expect that they will come with you, in solidarity?

When we talk about the barricades, they ask: 'Was it not there?' When we talk about the silence, they say: 'Was it not there?' When we curse the rising culture of barricading, they say: 'When was it not there?' When we talk about freedom, they ask: 'When were we free?' You talk about the post-truth, they ask when was truth?

---

[9] Translation of '*Mohanjodaro ki akhiri sidhi se*' (From the Last Stair of Mohenjo-daro). Ramashankar Yadav 'Vidrohi', *Nayi Kheti* (Allahabad: Jan Sanskriti Manch, 2011), 18.

The situation has worsened. It is the excess that we can see now. What is so new? The alarming situation was already there for the lowest rung. It is there. Ambedkar underlined the symptoms in his writings provocatively by saying how 'Hindus have fouled the air all over and everybody is infected, Sikh, Muslim and Christian'.[10] We cannot reclaim politics when cultural reflexes are infected. You cannot reclaim history when memories are purged. We cannot claim the body when the gaze is infected. You cannot deliberate on freedom of expression when others remain enslaved. Society must think of the 'we' from points of susceptibility, from the standpoints of the exposed; otherwise, the 'we' will remain a suspect.

So, what is the 'we' that we are talking about? You are looking for a dialogue when you come to the limit, to the edge. As we all are pushed to the limit, there is a possibility for a dialogue from the edge. Let's think from the barricades, let's start from the brink, let's think from the edge, let's think from the end.

Breathing with the End

Breathlessness presents the situation of breathing in the extreme, in severity, at a bare minimal level, in the shortage of air. It is breathing in despair, it is thinking viscerally. It is exasperating love for life. It is a call to freedom even in the condition of death. Breathing is the only thing one can think of at that moment. It is not breathing with the OM but breathing with the end. It is the condition in which dyspnoea and dystopia conspire together to shock us at daybreak and in the dark.

We all breathe but do not think about it unless it is under siege, unless we feel the shortage of air. We cannot think of living without breathing. It is fundamental to life. Once it stops, we cease to exist as living beings. Breathing, in a way, brings sensations of life and perceptions of freedom. It is fundamental to sensibilities. It is the primal force of all experiences. Breathing is not just about

---

[10] B.R. Ambedkar, *BAWS*, Vol. 1, 80.

yawning, coughing, and sneezing. It is also about the apparatus of speech, laughter, and languages that make freedom of expression possible. It enacts the first and the last movement of the body. It sets the first condition of freedom. The condition is simple: whether one can breathe freely or not. The denial of breathing is the denial of all rights and freedom.

In the true realms of rights and freedom, breathing is not about breathing in and breathing out; it is about freeing in and freeing out. It is about the path of circulation that circulates more air than we breathe. The BLM movement has proved that it is a battle between suffocating and not getting suffocated. In the precise moment of breathlessness, breathing comes as a force. Mimetic in its movement and visceral in its presence, it moves like a spirit in the dark. At this moment of the inability to breathe, one breathes with full guts, with gravitational force, with the energies of the sky. One breathes as the world breathes; one breathes as though it will be their last breath. An act of breathing becomes a force of transformation. This is the moment when Audre Lorde asks us to turn fears into fire. She came at full force in the severity of illness: 'I am going to write fire until it comes out my ears, my eyes, my noseholes — everywhere. Until it's every breath I breathe. I'm going to go out like a fucking meteor!'[11] The extreme presents a problem and a challenge for scholars, activists, and empathetic readers, for those who want to breathe freely and believe in transformative politics, and for us who think this moment has to end.

We can gape into the symptomatic condition of 'I Can't Breathe' — the slogan of the BLM movement, which is increasingly becoming a generic condition of life in many parts of the world. The question arises as to why there is a specific mention of the coronavirus when we can discuss the condition without it. It is important because the situation of 'I can't breathe' remains imperceptible in the dead conscience of a hierarchical society. You

---

[11] Audre Lorde, *A Burst of Light: And Other Essays* (New York: Ixia Press, 2017), 128.

see, but you don't see it, or you see it so much that the ways of seeing cease to exist. The familiar visuals kill visual perception.

Despite being invisible, the coronavirus created visibility. It produced a condition of estrangement. Hence, it enables us to think about things that remain invisible. It does it through a powerful mimetic presence. What others veiled in everydayness, Covid-19 showed it in its full nakedness. Can we think of a more naked slogan than '*Samajik doori ka samman karen*' (Respect the social distance) in a caste society? What everydayness could not show, the pandemic showed in an epic way. It is like creating an epic model of theatre from the everyday street scenes in a Brechtian sense. In the everydayness of caste society, the pandemic offers us an estranged model to see things from the outside. The connection, thus, becomes vital. Though the pandemic of Covid-19 is not the real site here, it is a powerful metaphor and reference point to think about life and freedom in a precarious situation.

Ishq (Love) and Risk

The connection between 'I can't breathe' and Covid-19 is also vital because the real capacity of a pandemic does not lie in the death and destruction it has caused, the people it has infected or killed, or in its global pandemic presence. Its vital performative capacity lies in the fear and panic it spreads. In other words, the virus is psychic, the pandemic is panic. The sense of risk goes more viral than the disease. Before it enters our body, it enters our psyche. And then, you cannot take the risk of not wearing a mask. One cannot take the risk of not maintaining distance. You cannot risk yourself when risk enters your relationship — the very name of the social. It becomes such a risky affair that you do not believe it to be imperative to give your consent to the state and the authorities. They like the way we operate. They do not think it is important to ask for your consent when you are already affected by the fear of risk.

The roles of the state and the citizen subjects were never as apparent as during this time of risk. It becomes obvious when we take an example of the Covid-19 lockdown and demonetization. Like a father, like a saviour, like a priest, the state takes us for a ride in the name of risk. We are thinking in the time of a risk economy that shapes the cultures and performances in the zones of confinement beyond the coronavirus.

Risk is central to thinking about totalitarian regimes and freedom. It emerges as the keyword in the encounter. The state curtails freedom by manufacturing risk, while the other risks the body for a more significant meaning of life and freedom. It is the playground on which the *ishq* (love) of the poet and the risk of power meet, for life and death, for rights and freedom, for the concealed repercussions, and for the unseen rebellion that will mark our future.

The ultimate defence that works in favour of the state and the authoritarian regime is the ideology of risk — attack, threat, and emergency. In this context, the Indian phrase of the 1970s, 'Emergency was imposed', becomes too real for any authoritarian regime. Read it literally. It says it all. There was no emergency, it was imposed. The regime plans the crisis, invents the risk, and creates the threat itself. Though we cannot say the same about the coronavirus, at least to the same degree, we cannot negate the rhetoric of risk either. Not to deny the threat of Covid-19. It was apocalyptic. Covid-19 invaded the security of the MOSSAD, the most secure and deadly security agency on earth. It threatened the capitalist world order. Yet, market capitalism soon contained the ideology of the virus in its favour.

The ideology was the risk. The regime performed the risk to curb rights and dissent. Let us note that the market ideology of risk always favours the authorities. Therefore, they keep giving us rhetoric: life without risk, love without risk, and sex without risk. Unsurprisingly, the coronavirus soon became the ally of neoliberal and authoritarian regimes. While the disease exposed the medical system of the market regime, this same regime sold the risk and bought consent to augment the authorities' power.

Amidst the pandemic, the authoritarian regimes of the world became more powerful. Risk and the regime soared together. Greater the risk, the greater the control of the regime, and the greater the authority! As the number of infections surged in India, the popularity of the Prime Minister soared. According to Morning Consult, a US-based survey and research firm, Prime Minister Modi's approval rating increased from 76 per cent to 83 per cent. Another study by the IANS-C-Voter showed that the trust in Modi's leadership jumped from 76.8 per cent on 25 March to 93.5 per cent as of 21 April 2020 amidst the rising cases of infections.[12] He is said to have become more powerful than he was ever before. With a bleached beard and saintly dress, Modi elevated his stature from a mundane leader to an extra-terrestrial figure who did not believe in interfering in the day-to-day affairs of the poor health system but maintained a special communication with the coronavirus. *Go Corona Go*, and coronavirus was gone. At the height of the humanitarian crisis, he performed the slogan: 'Turn crisis into an opportunity'. The slogan symbolizes the master catchphrase of the neoliberal ideology of risk. In this political manoeuvring, Covid-19 becomes the site of the unravelling of the problem of 'when we can't breathe'.

Symptoms and Suspensions

'When We Can't Breathe' is the sign and symptom of the curtailment of life and freedom. The symptom shows a condition that is close, but it is not a closure yet. It has not yet reached a dead end. Unlike closure, curtailment is still a process. It is a movement towards closure that can be interrupted. The barricade is there, but it can be crossed. Despite its moment of despair, it is a condition

---

[12] Bloomberg, 'PM Modi's popularity soars amid India's Covid fight', *Times of India*. 30 April 2020, https://timesofindia.indiatimes.com/india/pm-modis-popularity-soars-amid-indias-covid-fight/articleshow/75466935.cms

in which you are still breathing. You are still alive. There is still hope. There is time to retreat. There is a time to interrupt. The body can still cross the barricades beyond life and death. Even in the death of a person, I can't breathe can become a rallying point, as we have seen in the case of George Floyd, Rohith Vemula, and the 2012 Delhi gang-rape case. At any time, bodies can emerge as an assembly, walk in alliances and move against closure, against the distance, as we have seen in the case of the farmers' protest in Delhi in 2020-21.

The sense of breathlessness is a moment of suspension. At that moment, what matters is not the lockdown but the deadlock — the impasse that one cannot announce. It becomes the rites of passage for both the authorities and the unauthorized — the migrants, minorities and those engaging in civil disobedience. How do we think about the deadlock situation when things do not move? Time stops. Space sucks. Death looms larger than life. The dream gets devilish, and thinking becomes a tyrannical act. You think, but you cannot move. It is like running away in a dream. You want to inhale the wind like a Chinese dragon, but you feel a lack of space. The present becomes so alarming that the future does not hold. Time appears suspended in the time and space contained within a place. The body is between life and death, and you and I fall in love in isolation. Thinking about social distance is like living without breathing. This happens more at the psychic level as things do not move. Every breath slows down time and distance and the day breaks down the spatial and temporal sovereignty of a nation.

The condition has come to the body; it has come to words; it has come to breaths. Once words become prey, mob lynching becomes a chilled-out game. Then the worst is not in the killing but the fun of the violence it enacts, the fear it creates for the future, and the freedom it curtails. It seems that mob violence and lynching were never so chilling and chilled-out games in the Republic. Mixed with lies, violent fun spreads faster than a smile. Oskar Verkaaik observes that in such a situation, violence becomes constitutive of group identity. In his view, it provides social solidarity to the violent group. A new politics is born purely based on blood and violence.[13] When you see this becoming politics in the twenty-first century, you feel suffocated.

We can sense the problem of breathing both from the points of freedom and barricades. Anyway, the ideas of freedom and barricades were never so far away; they were just a body apart. Even when one falls on the barricade, one strengthens the notion of freedom. Borders not only separate, they are also connecting points. Freedom and barricades look for each other as a hunter looks for its prey. Both often meet on the walls, on the fences, on the window, bodies suspended like bats on the barricades shouting slogans of freedom and gallows marking the sign of resistance on the neck. One is right to think from the viewpoint of freedom as Arundhati Roy does in *Azadi*. I would like to sense it from the points of the barricades, the points of curtailments, and the zones of confinements, or as John Berger would say from the landmark of the prison: 'across the planet, we are living in a prison.'[14]

Between Necessity and Freedom

'I can't breathe', writes Rob Kyff, 'reflects the deeply rooted association between the act of breathing and the universal right to freedom, democracy and human dignity'.[15] We cannot deny these associations, but it is fundamentally a question of necessity. Breathing is perhaps the last act and a desperate plea for life and freedom. It is a matter of life and existence — the prerequisite of life. The migrant labourers were not asking for better wages or working conditions. They were looking for a meal for a day, a roof under

---

[13] Oskar Verkaaik, 'Fun and Violence: Ethnocide and the Effervescence of Collective Aggression', *Social Anthropology* 11, no. 1 (2003), 4.

[14] John Berger, *Meanwhile* (London: Drawbridge Books, 2008), 2.

[15] Rob Kyff, 'Breathing and freedom go together, but we need more than metaphors', *Hartford Courant*, 20 January 2021, https://www.courant.com/opinion/op-ed/hc-op-kyff-breathe-justice-0621-20200621-qyc4m55r3vhmhaxhtbzhzve7sm-story.html

which to stay. They wanted to meet their families in the apocalyptic crisis. They were not participating in a political movement. They wanted to leave as they lost their jobs. They wanted to move as migrants move from the villages to the cities. They move as the rail becomes a metaphor for their lives, and their lives are reduced to the movement from one city to another endlessly.

Farmers from Punjab were not asking for liberty and freedom. They were fighting to defend their life and sustenance. The questions of *Jal, Jangal, Jameen* (Water, Forest, and Land) for the Adivasis are not questions of love and freedom but a matter of survival. When one is asking for better air, one is not asking for luxury but life itself.

Marx differentiates between 'the realm of necessity' and 'the true realm of freedom'. He says that the realm of freedom 'by its very nature' lies beyond the sphere of material production and thus beyond the realm of necessity.[16] In a very Marxian sense, the slogan *'bhookhmari se azadi'* (freedom from hunger) becomes an oxymoron. Thus, we can say that the questions of *roti, kapda, aur makan* (food, cloth, and shelter) are not questions of freedom but matters of necessity. They are legal, moral, and social claims. They are the basis of the civil contract between the liberal state and the citizen subject. The state has been constantly breakings this social contract in present times.

But there comes a point when the realm of necessity and the realm of freedom come together. It happens in two moments. When right or the realm of necessity acquires an intrinsic value and freedom becomes a question of life and liberty. For women and migrants, it may start with a walk, but when a walk becomes a political statement against the imposition of the lockdown, then what was the realm of necessity enters into the realm of freedom. In this light, it would be antithetical to reduce the walk of the migrant labourers to the realm of necessity. They also walked with

16 Karl Marx. *Capital*, Vol. 3 (New York: International Publishers, 1977).

a larger sense of freedom and movement. It reminds me of Maya Krishna Rao's performance *Walk* during the protests against the 2012 Delhi rape case.

> Not 10, not 11
> 12 / midnight /
> *raat ke barah baje* / midnight,
> I want to walk

Rao's walk collapses the boundaries between the realm of necessity and the true realm of freedom. In this case, walking does not remain a necessity, it becomes an act of resistance. It becomes an allegory for freedom. It does not remain a matter of breathing but breathing as freedom.

Guts, Grits, and Life

Every day you hope for better. Every day you see a new low. A new sense of anxiety. A bolstered sense of curtailment. Every day you feel squeezed and narrowed down in your own body and geography. Young women who were fighting to open the lockup were locked up. One who advocated hate was out on the streets, and many who supported peace during the anti-CAA-NRC protests were booked for the riot. Rights have come to the point of defence. Instead of demands, you are asked to save whatever you can save — institutions, constitutions, universities, open spaces, land, graves, and dignified death.

But amidst this hopelessness, the condition of 'I can't breathe' articulates the resistance openly, such as the grit to live, the guts to fight, and to laugh in the face of a dictator. When one says 'I can't breathe', then what remain ineffable are the prefixes and suffixes that fully suffice that sentence. One who utters it always addresses it to somebody. You are not only saying you can't breathe. You indirectly say, 'Please get me out of here, I can't breathe. I can't breathe in this house. I can't breathe in your city, in your village, in your spaces, in your universities. You want to say that your theories are constraining; your knowledge is suffocating. Please get me out from here.' In such a situation, they make both pleas and resistance. A plea because they are vulnerable, and resistance because the act carries injustice.

The three words — 'I can't breathe' or 'we can't breathe' — are unparalleled in their evocation. It is rare to find such words that can match the elocution of oppression as they do. The yelling sound echoes the chord perhaps deeper than *nada* (the unstuck sound). It brings anger and compassion together, empathy and mobilization. I can't breathe as my biological body moves to the ideological body and becomes the allegory of life and freedom. The slogan, in Ben Okri's words, 'hints at the apocalypse of human values'.[17] It brings two questions together: what it means to be human and what it means to be inhuman. It is the outcry of the human being in one of its barest conditions. Okri says, '"I can't breathe" goes beyond saying that you are depriving me of freedom, of humanity, of respect. It says: you are depriving me of the right to air itself'. Perhaps, the fundamentals of the human condition cannot go deeper than this elocution.

Against Floyd's repeated plea, Police officer Derek Chauvin shouted, 'Then stop talking, stop yelling, it takes a heck of a lot of oxygen to talk'.[18] What happens when yelling is banned, crying is banned, and mourning is banned? Despite Chauvin's warning, Floyd repeated that he could not breathe. The mind gives up, but the body resists, and when the body gives up, the word resists.

---

[17] Ben Okri, '"I Can't Breathe": Why George Floyd's Words Reverberate Around the World', *The Guardian*, 8 June 2020. https://www.theguardian. com/commentisfree/2020/jun/08/i-cant-breathe-george-floyds-words-reverberate-oppression

[18] Richard A. Oppel Jr. and Kim Barker, 'New Transcripts Detail Last Moments for George Floyd', *New York Times*, 8 July 2020. https://www.nytimes. com/2020/07/08/us/george-floyd-body-camera-transcripts.html

There is no other corporeal moment in which all limbs come together in such a synesthetic way. It is the condition in which breathing and resisting come so close. If we can't breathe implies the absolute sense of confinement, it also brings about the fundamental meaning of resistance.

Like the allegorist who finds meanings even in wreckage and ruin, I am trying to find meanings in confinement, in death, in disappearance, in detention of life when the body becomes more evocative and breathing more powerful. It is the situation that turns the body into a powerful allegory. When the air becomes electric. And every breath matters as a matter of life and death. Walter Benjamin would say that allegory is a way of seeing any object, image, or text as multivalent, multi-faceted, and polysemic.[19] The situation of breathlessness produces a similar multivalent, multifaceted, polysemic condition in which the body resonates like an instrument.

Body on the barricades becomes an allegory for thinking about the limits on freedom, the shrinking spaces, the dying democracy, and the barricades full of iron nails. This is not about the limits of thoughts, but about thinking from (*what could be*) limited thoughts. If the former is an opening, the other is closure. One is lightening, the other is darkening, moving slowly and switching off the lights one by one. Imagine a theatre situation where the actors are slowly disappearing, and the stage is slowly getting dark to disappear in the darkness of the night. In this precise moment, our body becomes all eyes. We enter the realm of extra-awareness. Our senses get fully activated, and the body more aware of its actions. Eyes see more in the darkness. The mind perceives more. We see faces staring from the walls. We hear sounds in deep silences. Body stands alert to defend itself from all possible assaults. It keeps vigil

---

[19] Alan Wall, 'Reflections on Walter Benjamin 7. Baudelaire, Allegory and the Aura', *Fortnightly Review*, 22 June 2015, https://fortnightlyreview. co.uk/2015/06/reflections-benjamin-7/

on the vigilantes. This darkness — the curtailment reminds us of the great Marxist Hindi poet Muktibodh's poem, *Andhere mein* (In the Dark). Here is a short excerpt from the longer poem:

In life's …
      dark chambers
         someone is pacing up and down
            ceaselessly;
I can hear the sound of his steps
again and again … again and again
I cannot see him … cannot see him
but he goes on wandering
Someone arrested in an enchanted cave
Someone unstoppable
      asserts his existence
         like the echo of deep mysterious
darkness,
resounding nearby, behind the wall.
And the beating of my heart
asks — Who is he
that I can hear, but cannot see?
Then bulging plaster
suddenly falls from the wall
Sand full of lime cracks
Flakes slip
a big face emerges
of its own accord
A silhouette appears on the wall –
Pointed nose,
magnificent brow,
firm chin;
An unknown unfamiliar shape.
Who is he

that I can see, but
cannot know!
    Manu?[20]

It is in this appearance, awareness, and alertness amidst curtailment and barricading, in the dark, we are looking for hope. It is in this hearing and disappearing, we are charting our path. We will rise, arise from the point of 'We can't breathe.'

---

[20] Muktibodh, *In the Dark: Andhere Mein*, translated by Krishna Baldev Vaid (New Delhi: Rainbow Publishers, 2001).

2. Words and Demagogues

What Demagogues Do With Words

It is important to remember that the Holocaust actually did not start from gas chambers. This hatred gradually developed from words, stereotypes and prejudices through legal exclusion, dehumanization and escalating violence.

— Auschwitz Memorial[1]

It isn't only Nazi actions that have to vanish, but also the Nazi cast of mind, the typical Nazi way of thinking, and its breeding ground: the language of Nazism.

— Victor Klemperer [2]

It appears odd to talk about words when people are lynched by mobs. But the assault on words is not isolated from the lynching in the streets. The assault on words and the assault on life are inseparable acts. Victims have to be labelled before they are lynched. Witches are branded before they are burnt. Authoritarianism must curtail words, before curtailing life and freedom.

This is what any authoritarian regime does! Words become the first casualty. Before they lynch the body, they lynch words. Before

---

[1] Auschwitz Memorial tweeted this message on 27 November 2018. See Corrine Purtill, 'The Auschwitz Museum Hits Back at Lindsey Graham's Holocaust Mansplaining', *Quartz*, 20 November 2018, https://qz.com/1476559/auschwitz-museum-hits-out-at-lindsey-grahams-holocaust-mansplaining/.

[2] Victor Klemperer, *The Language of the Third Reich* (London: Continuum, 2007), 2.

they diminish life and freedom, they diminish meanings and metaphors. Before they take democracy for a ride, they talk about 'too much democracy'.[3] They seize criticisms with slogans and critics with clamour. They turn words toxic so they can perform hate. Words lose their capacity to heal and mourn. Soothing turns into scorn. The curtailment of words doesn't end here. The politics that starts with hate ultimately leads to genocide and crimes against humanity.

Demagogues command in monologues and lay siege on the very capacity of the words. They use words to monopolize the media and market. They organize them to monopolize legal and moral discourses. They arrange them to take control of debates and discourses. They utilize them to manipulate figures and statistics. They strategize them to monopolize violence, silence and stratagem. They deploy them to dominate the definition of people and democracy.

Rising authoritarianism slowly swallows up the spaces of dialogue. Like a dialogue — the breathing space of language dies its death. Demagogues enter spaces like a killer speaking in the language of a saint. Slowly, they take control of everything we can think of: politics, culture, media, religion, and education. The more they take control, the more they want. With an approach of totalitarianism at the top, there is no stop. Demagoguery enters other spheres of life as well. The space of dialogue gradually shrinks, and we can only hear a monologue from the top. Rising demagoguery in contemporary India is a sign that the dialogue has shrunk. The spirit of communication is reaching a dead end. In such situations, the news anchor speaks like a spokesperson of the ruling party. The media barks not against power, but against the weak and the dissenters. If crowds enjoy the fun of violence, the media finds its solace in voyeuristic pleasure in the incitement

---

[3] Amitabh Kant, CEO of the public policy think tank NITI Aayog, in 2020 offered 'Too much democracy' as the reason why, according to him, tough reforms are difficult in India.

of violence. The fun of violence also enters our language.

The power of a demagogue rests in words. It lies in 'promises' and 'performances' of speeches. It lies in the slogans that shut up any arguments. It lies in their lies, and in twisted tales that they deliver as a monologue. It lies in the very promises of democracy: in 'people's power', 'people's leader', 'people's aspiration', 'people's museum'. This does not mean that our existing world of words is perfect. Our usages are not ideal. They are a product of social relations, caste, gender, race, and other hierarchies. We all know how *gaalis* (abuses) target women and lower castes in India.

We need to have critical approaches to words. We need to subvert power and hierarchies embodied in it. We need to reinvent them in all possible ways, as many poets and philosophers did in their words and verses without liquidating creative energies. Before we discuss the rising culture of demagoguery and curtailment of words, let's discuss the deep meaning and creative power of words.

Creative Power of Words

O shabdan tero naam hazaron, kya vani kya bol
O words you reverberate in thousand names,
Some call you voice, some call you utterance.[4]

What is a word? A definition cannot hold it. From where does it emerge? It springs on labour's rhythm, lovers' tongues, in poets' minds, and sufferers' screams. It is an imaginative body of longing and desire. On the one hand, it is an abstraction from bodies. On the other hand, it is a concretization of the forms of embodied life. Poets and writers strive for it. But they also drown in it. One who tries to understand words, surrenders to them; one who doesn't, simply follows them. Words are the ultimate *guru*. Poets seek liberation in them.[5] Intellectuals want proficiency in them. It is the

[4] Anonymous.
[5] Sufis and Bhaktis are popular mystic traditions in India that played an important role in the shaping of language and popular culture in medieval

liberatory capacity of words that make them omnipotent across cultures and communities. It is the creative power of words that diminishes with demagoguery.

Perhaps no other schools of Indian thought have understood the profundity of the word as the Bhaktis and the Sufis. For them, a word is a *dhvani* (sound) that pervades the body and the universe. It is a *vachana* (promise) made to the god and beloved. It is a *pramana* (evidence) of truth and love. It is the *zameer* (essence) and the *mool* (root) of life and existence. It is the only testimony that stands for truth. It is a repertoire that keeps records like oracle bones. It is an unparalleled repository of memories and the archive of human civilization.

Words are figures beyond the rhetoric of speeches. They are characters performing their roles. They have their potency. They have their personalities. They move in a specific way. They behave in a particular style. They form a particular association with objects, spaces and individuals. They are meant to perform a particular task. They inhale and exhale their own time and space. They pause. They move. They feel. They rest. They manifest. They become the manifestos of our lives and freedom.

Words are not about what we see on the page. As we see them, they move to us, they converse with us. They start a dialogue. They become alive in our hearts, ears and eyes. They animate objects and give life to the inanimate world. They give names to the nameless world. Stories move the stranded forest. In the absence of figures and physical evidence, they become the proof — a sign of our existence. They create a bridge between silences and utterances. A deep scream can create a hole in history. An utterance can create a space in the universe. When they move, mountains move; they move in the sound of the cloud thunder; they move in silence too.

Words in the form of sounds diversify our space and environment. Hear the chirping sounds of birds and crickets.

---

and pre-modern India.

Hissing sounds of snakes. Gossips of the objects that you can't hear. What is a sound? Shape, body, or a scale of a noise? Do we understand the songs of locusts? Sometimes, sound takes the shape of the body. Sometimes, bodies melt into words. The body becomes the vessels that resonate like *mridunga* (drum). To understand a world, not only is embodiment important, but also 'emwordiment' — a state when bodies become words.[6] Do bodies travel through the voice? Do they feel separated in the sound? Where do they long, if not in the songs? What is the song of separation all about, if not bodies meeting in words? What is the song of union, if it is not words melting bodies and making it one?

The body becomes the basis of many of our musical instruments. What is a tambourine? Body, words, or echoes? On one occasion, bodies become a set of musical instruments — more than a drum set. Each limb can resonate. It can roar like a tiger; it can cry like a cricket. It can sing like a tambourine. The stomach does not go silent when it is upset. It growls. It makes a noise: '*gurgurgur*'. On the other occasion, the body becomes a *patra* (empty vessel) into which words and sound can enter.

One can discuss the different dimensions of the body, words and their association with life. Words remain vital to life and the world. *Naad, nama,* and *kalma* are their few names. They are the creators of the universe. They are perhaps the most beautiful creations of human beings. Song, music, poetry, writings, carvings — words have many forms and none. They can be formless and merely a concept. They can be shapeless and merely a sound. They can be symbols or merely a sign. How do we read the sound that arises with human cries but fails to take any shape? They can end up as strings of echoes that do not produce meanings but keep resonating. Even without physical forms, they can touch the innermost organs. When injured, they can crawl into our bones and stick to the skin with or without leaving any mark.

---

[6] I heard this term first from the Kannada poet H.S. Shivaprakash, who contrasts it with embodiment.

The vitality of the word is of utmost significance. The problem is not that we do not know this. The problem is that everyone knows this — dictators as well as dissenters, poets as well as politicians. Thus, words become the site of conflicts. They are used in wars, they are used to inflict pain. They are used to denigrate others. They are deployed to announce the war. They are the most potent weapon for rabble-rousers. Listen to the words in the cries of warmongers.

In the Indian tradition, the most fundamental conflict does not lie between the text and the oral tradition but between textuality and orality. Words are still part of the oral tradition unless they are textualized. Though texts are an arrangement of words, we can't reduce words to text. Though some texts can kill the spirit of words, within the texts, some words can function as breathing points. Though they are part of each other, the relationship between words and texts is the most contentious one. Kabir criticized the pundits. He criticized the Vedas and other textual traditions, saying:

> Reading books upon books, the world died
> and none became wise.
> Four letters: love
> Read those and be wise.

Yet he held onto words — the two and a half words of *prem* (love). In fact, he used *shabda* (words) to attack the *shastra* (textual authority). Those words are not merely a device. They are not rhetoric. They carry a deeper meaning. Words, breaths, bodies, and spaces are interwoven into each other like a weaver's clothes. Suspended in threads, connected through lines, dyed in colours, baked in clay, they become a *ghat* — the dancing pot in the river.

Though several saints and poets were against texts, they were rarely against words. They saw the creation, power, and wisdom in them. They saw *jiva* (life) in words that animated the life forces.

For them, words were the site of world-making. Sufis and saints perceived the echoes of words pervading the universe through the *naad* (the unstuck sound). It is through words that poets created their life world. They saw words as characters dancing on the canvas. They themselves became words to enter the hearts of gods and lovers. They say it all began with words — in the very act of naming — when the unnamed was named. *Nama* (a word) was the nemesis of creation.[7] Saints and Faqirs sang in praise of *nama* — an act of constant naming.

Words have a much deeper significance for poets, healers, and philosophers. They become the carrier of their lives and messages. For them, the word is the soul of creative power. It is the site where creation begins and ends. It is a connecting principle between you, me, and the world. It has the magical power of transformation. It arises in the poet Faiz Ahmad Faiz's eternal slogan of *Anal-Haq* — a state of annihilating one's ego that brings us together, and that makes us both — I and you too. In the song of saint Tuka, words are *abhanga* — one that is indestructible. In the song of Telugu balladeer Gaddar, they are *taragani*, inexhaustible and boundless. Words exist in ideal form here. Boundlessness is the ideal of the words.

Words have supreme place in the magico-ritual world. Shamans heal through them, magicians strike through them, devotees invoke their gods through them. Shamans call upon forests and mountains and hear the river's call to understand their pain and suffering. Great activists and philosophers who dreamt about changing the world were quite sensitive in their usages. Words were like pearls in their threads. They used words as life — a living and moving force. They were stringing words together as they were stringing the broken pieces of their lives and struggles.

---

[7] Rama is merely a name resounding Nama in Bhakti and other practices. It is a different story that the figure of Rama has taken over *nama* in many songs, music, and performing traditions, reducing more powerful manifestations of *nama*.

People say that Walter Benjamin rarely used words unnecessarily. Karl Marx's writings interweave life and words so intricately that the readers wonder whether they are reading a text or a life. Jean-Paul Sartre's deployment of words shows his quest for freedom and truth. Ambedkar's call to annihilate caste is not only an attack on the caste system but also an onslaught on the words that sustain and perform it in our everyday lives. If Maya Angelou's words give us wings to fly, Toni Morrison's words offer us healing. They are rhythm and resonance, finding meanings in the *bol* (utterances). They are bodies finding names in the world. They are strings resonating in the bodies. They are sounds pulsating in the blood. They are footprints marking history in the absence of an archive.

For activists and philosophers, words are full of life and action. The power and authority can imprison the bodies, but words can go beyond enclosures and perform the tasks of freedom. When borders remain closed, they can cross boundaries. India and Pakistan have filled their frontiers with armies and tanks, but they could not stop the songs and music that cross the boundaries. The words of Kabir and the voice of Abida Parveen do not see boundaries. Nazim Hikmet wrote some of his best poems from within the prison walls. But the words came out. Hikmet's poetry, in John Berger's words, 'contained more space than any poetry [...]. They didn't describe space; they came through it, they crossed mountains.'[8]

While politics is not just about words, words do play an important role. It is the word that imagines the alternative world in the first instance. Martin Luther King Jr's speech, 'I have a dream' came in words before it split onto the streets. The racist ideology couldn't tolerate his transformative words. He was killed, and so many others. From Narendra Dabholkar to Govind Pansare, M.M. Kalburgi to Gauri Lankesh. Many were poisoned, many imprisoned, many persecuted in other ways. The word becomes a

[8] John Berger, *Hold Everything Dear: Dispatches on Survival and Resistance* (New York: Pantheon Books, 2007), 45.

question of life and death, both for the activists and the authorities. They are compelling statements on life. Amidst threats, words have to be nourished for life and freedom. For all these reasons, words need our attention in the rising culture of authoritarianism, which perverts the meaning and essence of words.

Words of the Demagogue

Demagogues not only instrumentalize words, they turn them against life. They curtail words and only allow them to perform certain tasks, often violent in nature. They twist the very essence of words. They make death gallows and genocidal labs to hang the words upside down, and to play linguicide. They engineer the words and desensitize them from their feelings and senses. Words are stripped down to their bodies and totalized to stand with the totalitarian regime. They are scratched from the wombs and pitted against their mothers from where they are born. Demagogues use words for their dead ends.

Do words suffer? Can they be coloured? Can they be coded? Can they be curtailed? Can they be emptied out from their souls? It is difficult. Yet, for the demagogues, this is not impossible. They can curtail words; they can cripple them. Words can be wronged; they can be wormed. They can be filled with hate. How do we see the meaning of the Republic after the coming of the Republic TV, a right-wing Indian news channel? By misconstruing words, there is an attempt to change the meaning of the public and the republic itself. Many political terminologies have gone through a radical transformation. Just imagine how democratic terms have changed in the last few years. Words such as 'republic', 'nation', and 'democracy' are twisted beyond the point of recognition. What happens when ideas are hollowed out and emptied of meaning? They are used as rhetoric. As democracy is reduced to election and perception, the rhetoric and the war of words become their legitimacy.

The war of words in recent years in Indian elections is not a poetic duel but an anti-poetic tirade. Leaders use them to mobilize people and elect themselves. Words create mobs; mobs create words. Words and mobs, mobs and words move together to seek the power and majority of the populist government. The deployment of words and slogans sets the new election apart from other elections. This is not something new. Riots before an election are not new. But there has been a drastic change over the years. The election campaign has turned into a hate campaign. It has pitted the majority community against the minority. Hatemongers are the star campaigners. The formula is clear: the more venom you spill on the streets, the more votes you guarantee on the strips. Hate mongers are the honoured guests in the election. A new breed has also arrived. They mix corporate culture with new religiosity. They spice up religion and add a vibrator to Bhakti. Hindutva pop grows on hate. They rob words. They rob songs and music. They rob slogans. They spit venom and turn politics into a stratagem.

Demagogues have changed the very sense of words. Some words have acquired new meanings that negate their own essence. We all know what has happened to beautiful words such as *faqir, jogi, sadhu,* and *bhakt.* A bhakt is supposed to be a partaker of a spiritual quest but now participates in trolling. They are calling fanatic words fantastic; they are trying to make them fashionable. They are poisoning them. The meanings are being twisted to generate a new force. Through this extreme distortion, the bhakts have crafted a cult of opposition to any form of knowledge. What happened to *vikas* (development), *mann ki baat* (inner thought), and *acche din* (good days)? Haven't they met a similar fate? One fundamental aspect of this manipulative word-making is a monologue. The demagogues extricate spaces of dialogue. They monologize them. They monopolize them for soliloquy. Despite their differences, all the demagogues love their voices. Their own voices become their greatest fantasy.

Birth of the Monologue

Any hierarchical society is a society of monologues. The husband speaks, and the wife listens. The priests speak, and the devotees listen. The guru speaks, and the pupils listen. The leaders speak, and the followers listen. The son follows the father's order. It does not mean that dialogue does not happen. A dialogue happens among the men, among the Brahmins, within the caste, in the castle and the streets, and within the quarantine boundaries. They remain a monologue in the real sense. The Indian public sphere is the best example of this monologue. The public sphere becomes the property of the same caste and class. A dialogue happens to maintain caste decorum.

A dialogue happens between a husband and wife too, but not on an equal footing. One orders, one obeys. There are lines — the *lakshman rekha* — a line of convention that shouldn't be crossed. Some are not supposed to raise their pitches in respect. Some words are not supposed to be heard, even in the dark? *Hey, did you say dic…ta…tor…? Who, I? … No … never.*

There won't be many takers if I say that the birth of the monologue goes back to the origin of Sanskrit poetry. The very 'first poem' — *maa nishaada* we praise, is a curse. It exists in the form of a true monologue. In the story, this occurs when a sage curses a hunter for killing one of the two birds that were engaged in amorous play. On witnessing the inconsolable grieving of the female bird, the poet's sorrow (*shoka*) resulted in a *shloka* (verse). Valmiki, the harbinger poet of Sanskrit literature, curses the hunter to suffer forever for his heinous crime. Of course, the poetry is not a real social representation. But we can't deny that the story is placed in the Brahminical imagination.

Dialogue does not occur between the poet and the hunter. It is a monologue. The sage didn't feel it important to ask the hunter why he killed the bird, as in the other case, the Buddha asked Angulimal, a murderer who used to wear the fingers of the killed, why he was engaging in heartless violence. The sage didn't feel it important to have a dialogue with the lower caste hunter. Such a dialogue cannot be imagined in a hierarchical social order. The caste order curtails the scope of a dialogic imagination.

The same poet who cursed the hunter showers praises on the killing and hunting expedition of King Rama. The formula is clear: the king has to be praised, and the hunter has to be cursed. Men and upper castes have to be praised, and women and Shudras become the target of curse words. Vedic violence is not violence, but non-Vedic violence has to be dealt with death. And remember, not everyone can curse. There are figures of moral and social authority, only whose curses work. Others can curse, but the utterances will not perform their act as they do not hold power and efficacy. A popular saying in north India goes that the witches' curses cannot even kill cats. Witches do not carry the weight of a king, a Brahmin, or a poet.

Everyone does not have the moral authority to abuse and curse. In the popular imagination, Brahmin priests, sages, gurus, and kings have the right to curse as they are the moral authority. They are the sacrosanct figures. One can also discuss the nature of the curse that adheres to the hierarchies. The curse does not make sense if you do not hold moral power. The purpose is to preserve dharma and the moral-social order. Upper-caste royal poetry was about adhering to Brahminical morality. The Hindu demagogue expects words to be like that. A curse is an extreme form of a monologue. Once it is out, it is out. It results from an extreme form of hate or an extreme sense of insecurity and fragility. Curses are becoming mainstream in the public culture of India. There are many examples where political leaders started their political careers with curses.

Another form of a curse comes from the oppressed section. They curse when they feel blocked, when they feel curtailed, when they feel choked, when they see that they are not getting justice. They pray for justice in the form of curses. These curses cannot be compared with those of sages who curse from privileged points of view or maintain certain moral standards. Abuse and curse words are closely related to class and gender, and that is the way they perform their tasks.

Unlike many Bhakti, Sufi, and subaltern traditions, *shabda* stands for *yasogiti* in Sanskrit language, a song praising one's fame. There has been a long tradition of singing *yasogiti* in Hindu India. What is expected from words is praise and not criticism. This is what demagogues expect from art and literature. They want to hear praise instead of criticism. There is no question of 'nindak niyare rakhiye' ('Keep critics in close proximity, so you don't miss the criticism') that Kabir and Rahim propagated.

Let's come back to the fundamental question — what does a demagogue do with words? I outline five points which are by no means exhaustive. First, demagogues are adept at extracting words from their established contexts. They give new colours to words. They cut words from daily life and struggles and transport them to divine and corporate realms. The best example is naming a person with disabilities or a differently abled body as *divyang* (divine body). Another aspect of this demagoguery is the marketing of words and language. It tries to convert words into the language of the market. It is often difficult to say whether they are words or 'ideas without words' (coined by Oswald Spengler). It is used as a mechanical and linguistic mechanism to create ready-made phrases and stereotypes.

As a true demagogue, Modi has a knack for creating populist false etymologies using acronyms. He creates *nomina sacra* (sacred names) through new symbolisms that resonate with a neo-conservative corporate culture. A telling example is Modi's acronym for the Mars Orbiter Mission — MOM. 'I was sure Mom won't disappoint us', said Modi after the mission's success. In one stroke, he stripped both the idea of the mission and the ideal of the mother. Words are fused together to form a conservative propaganda motif.

Second, when demagogues speak in a monologue, the words often serve as nothing but cannon fodder. They shut up any space for dialogue and eliminate the possibility of debate. Demagogues and rabble-rousers use poisonous invectives to paralyze reasoned arguments.

Third, demagogues perform incantations on the emerging public sphere to fantasize the masses. Today they perform incantations such as the chants of '*Jai Shri Ram*' ('Glory to Lord Rama') in the parliament. Leaders use them to deflect the masses from reasoned deliberation. Incantations in the form of curses or maledictions aim to intimidate the truth. Words don't remain unaffected when they are used for cursing. In the process, they are also poisoned and drained of their energies. They become hunting fields for the mobs.

Fourth, demagogues tend to be ruthless slayers of words. They throttle words in quite unbelievable ways. If they want to kill the *shabda* (word) of Kabir, they invoke Kabir in a way that conjures away the essence of everything the saint-poet said. If they want to kill the spirit of Ambedkar's politics, they invoke his words in a way that they become unrecognizable. When the demagogue speaks about the farmers' concerns, one can take it for granted that farmers are under attack. The act of invocation becomes a ritual act of sacrifice in which the invoked figure has to be either sacrificed or contained.

Finally, while the power of demagogues rests on claims of transforming the system, they are, in reality, afraid of any change that would genuinely serve the people and, thus, this makes their posturing redundant. The demagogues zealously guard their public image that they carefully construct through words. Words have given them the ability to project a false aura of selflessness and sacrifice. Toni Morrison beautifully said, 'fascism talks ideology but it is really just marketing — marketing for power'.[9]

---

[9] Toni Morrison, *Mouth Full of Blood: Essays, Speeches, Meditations* (London: Vintage, 2020), 36–37.

The demagogue dreads any challenge to this image-mongering.

Such a challenge, of course, requires many things. The foremost among them is the task of reclaiming words and their usage from the cynical sway of demagoguery. Our poets, writers, and activists would have to play a key role. They would have to reclaim words, not just by restoring and reinventing their worlds of meaning but also by clearing away the dangerous curses and incantations that menace the public sphere today.

Demagogues also bring the language of genocide to the centre. What we call the language of genocide is not about the death of a language. It is not a case of linguicide. It is not about the grafting of one language over others. It is about implanting gratification on language. It is about the use of hate music to perpetuate the genocidal spiral.

The language of genocide generates hateful words. It creates labels that make violence possible. It labels and dehumanizes specific communities. The state uses pathological words in which 'distancing' and 'sanitization' acquire social meanings. Words like 'purification', 'disease', 'contamination', and 'treatment' have already entered the social and public spheres of our day-to-day lives. Once these terms become part of our society, we can carry the genocide without the demagogues and demigods in power.

Writer Arundhati Roy has pointed out that these are not casual usages. She describes the process by which the language of genocide enters our landscape. She writes, "'Infest/infestation" implies disease/pests. Diseases must be cured. Pests must be exterminated. Maoists must be wiped out. In these creeping, innocuous ways, the language of genocide has entered our vocabulary'.[10]

If Adivasis are called worms, parasites, and pests, Muslims are called snakes in green attire, and those who are to be eliminated. Several battalions engaged in India's para-military offence against the so-called Maoists — Operation Green Hunt — are

---

[10] Arundhati Roy, 'Walking with the Comrades', *Outlook India*, 29 March 2010.

named Cobra and Greyhounds, following the logic of beasts for beasts. Slavoj Žižek's remark is important here. He underlines that if language gets infected by violence, which occurs under the influence of contingent 'pathological' circumstances, then it distorts the inherent logic of symbolic communication.[11]

On the other side, the form of violence enacted through words perpetuates cultural injustices. They make their presence felt on memory and the landscape. Such incrimination of language has long-time negative effects. Such words help the state and authority maintain their monopoly on violence. People perceive themselves, their relationships, their future with others, and the world through language. Words, in this case, have an enormous effect as they inject fear and inferiority complexes into the lives of individuals and communities. The form of violence creates a superiority complex in one section and an inferiority complex in the other section.

Subverting the Subverter

When it comes to words, Kabir was an iconoclast. He shattered the existing use of words and languages based on hierarchies. He tried to free the words from rituals, scriptures, structures, and language too. He turned the language upside down to connect to the lower orders.

He inspired the marginalized sections to speak out, write poetry, sing songs, and have a dialogue. He firmly stood against religious and cultural hegemony. He showed the transformative power of words and what one can do with words. He criticized both Hindus and Muslims for their religiosity. He challenged the *Vedas* and the *Quran*. His followers, the *Kabirpanthi*, who largely come from the subaltern sections of both the Hindu and Muslim communities, criticized the priestly traditions of both religions.

I was shocked when I heard that Narendra Modi, who is known

---

[11] Slavoj Žižek, *Violence: Six Sideways Reflections* (New York: Picador, 2009), 61.

for his hateful politics, was going to offer homage to the saint-poet. In an extreme act of demagoguery, Modi went to appropriate Kabir. What would be the meaning of that appropriation? A demagogue appropriating Kabir can be seen as a subversion of subversion. While the act looks like subversion, it ultimately establishes a hierarchy by emptying out the very act of subversion. The act shows how far a demagogue can go towards killing the power of words. Kabir stands for the ethos of words. A demagogue not only scuttles the spaces of dialogue, he also attempts to scuttle the figure who stands for its ethos. That being the case, Kabir was the target.

By subverting words, Kabir subverted the ways of seeing the world. Here is an example of his extreme subversion:

Who will be sheriff [judge]
In a town littered with meat
Where the watchman
Is a vulture? [...]
Frog sleeping
Snake on guard;
Bull giving birth
Cow sterile
Calf milked
Lion forever leaping
To fight the jackal.
Morning, noon and night;
Kabir says, rare listeners
Hear the song right.[12]

Modi's attempt to appropriate Kabir was indeed a daring act. It aimed to subvert the ultimate subverter — the iconoclast. Let's not get confused. Modi's act of subversion was not a radical act. In its essence, it was an extremely conservative act. By subverting Kabir,

[12] Linda Hess and Sukhdeo Singh, *The Bijak of Kabir* (New York: Oxford University Press, 2002), 73.

Modi wanted to straighten away what Kabir had subverted.

Modi wanted to make Kabir's words plain. His act of subversion was a case of perversion. It was pathological. It was an offence to the words and ideals of the saint-poets who fought against the same divisive ideology that Modi and his ilk represent. But Modi did what he is known for doing the best. He misinterpreted the history and legacy of Kabir, standing right beside the saint's birthplace in Banaras and his burial ground in Maghar in Uttar Pradesh. How do we read Modi's homage to Kabir? His attempt to appropriate Kabir is to dumb down his complex words and teachings. The right-wing conservative interpretation aims to straighten the extreme subversion embodied in Kabir's deep quest.

Sheriff and watchman, mouse and vulture, cow and calf, lion and jackal — these human and non-human figures are extreme metaphors in Kabir's poetry. More than figures, they reveal the philosophy. The poem is part of the rich repertoire of Kabir's *ulatbansi* (upside-down language). The form of poetry is also known as *ulta bani*, the discourse that goes against the tide. Modi, in his offering, attempted to fix these metaphors to their dead ends. He tried to narrow down everything around Kabir to one interpretation, making traditions straightforward and absolute.

Kabir's upside-down language is a case of remarkable reversal. He asks us to see the world after subverting the existing relationships. I see in Kabir's *ulatbansi* a deep sense of queering. Queering here stands for a perspective that challenges the normative and hetero-normative modes of thinking. Without fixing positions, it changes the hierarchies of 'up' and 'down', 'high' and 'low', 'pure' and 'impure', and 'human' and 'animal'. He reverses the usual roles and relations in which the frog sleeps, and the snake sits on guard. The bull gives birth, and the cow goes sterile. He carries the subversion of all aspects of life through words. He sings,

It's all one skin and bone
one piss and shit

one blood, one meat
From one drop, a universe
Who's Brahmin? Who's Shudra?[13]

For all these reasons, Kabir's path becomes difficult, not only for the conservatives, but for the progressives too. Kabir's path is not easy. The Sufi saint-poet clearly says to his followers:

I've burned my house down
The torch is in my hand.
Now I'll burn down the house of anyone
Who wants to follow me.[14]

Who would want to follow Kabir with such a strenuous warning? Following the path of Kabir with conviction is a commitment one would rarely like to make. Rather, appropriating Kabir is much easier. The tradition of appropriating Kabir began during his lifetime. So much so that various communities fought over his dead body, staking their claim over the deceased saint. Instead of Kabir's ideology, they were more interested in accommodating Kabir into their respective ideologies. The same can be said to be happening in our demagogues' love for Kabir. They want to appropriate Kabir into the Hindutva ideology. They want to use his words to attack Muslim religious practices but idealize his Hinduism.

By misinterpreting and erasing Kabir's radical language and philosophy, Modi wanted to accommodate him as part of his Hindutva ideology. His homage to Kabir was an extraneous performative act that declared Kabir dead and normalized what Kabir had reversed and criticized through his words and actions.

Kabir left Banaras and went to Maghar to break the city's Brahminical ideals. There was a belief that one who dies in Banaras

13 Hess and Singh, *The Bijak of Kabir*, 19.
14 Hess and Singh, *The Bijak of Kabir*, 5.

directly gets *moksha* (liberation). As an iconoclast, Kabir chose not to die in Banaras. He instead chose Maghar, a site of hell. Modi went from Kashi to Maghar only to represent the philosophy and ideals of Kashi in Maghar. He went to Maghar, keeping the same Banaras in his heart and mind. With the same heart and mind, he wants to transform Kabir for the service of his own ideology.

Kabir lived and worked in Banaras, but he was never a part of the city. The Kashi (Banaras) of Kabir and the Kashi of pandits remain quite apart from each other. Right-wing ideology attempts to show that the city is sans fractures and faultiness, to present a sewer as a river that smoothly flows from one side to the other. The point is not that both sides do not meet and flow but that they often meet in confrontation. The current goes against the tide.

Saint-poets warned against the use of words for self-praise. Kabir said that utter only such words that are deprived of all your bodily pride. But what happens when words are used to express bodily pride and power pride (a 56-inch chest)? Modi's speeches are full of the words of achievements and the language of conquerors.

We wish that demagogues would have truly believed in Kabir's words. But then, they would not have remained the same. It would have been a remarkable transformation of a demagogue to a person of dialogue. They would have sung like Kabir breaking all forms of hierarchies.

> First of all, I was born
> then my elder brother
> With pomp and show
> my father was born
> last of all, my mother![15]

As authoritarianism comes to curtail life and freedom at every level, it is vital to understand the curtailment of breath and words

---

[15] M. Ali and M. Ram, *Kabir in Rajasthan: 13 Folk Songs of Kabir* (Bangalore: The Kabir Project, Srishti School of Art, Design & Technology, 2008), 30.

together. Before anything else falls, words fall prey to demagogues. We need to understand that words must be disfigured before the people and communities are. But demagoguery doesn't end here; it enters into the blood and ultimately asks for sacrifice.

What we are witnessing is the extreme curtailing of words. Meaningful words are turned upside-down. Speeches are turning into monologues. Words that used to be a soothing balm have been turned into bombs. The songs of hope whirl into helplessness and despair. The slogans that used to drive change now erect walls. The slogans of victory end up in terror and destruction. The disposed hear displacement when the authority debates development. The demagogues use the words like cultural bombs to annihilate people's belief in themselves.

Words have been the real captives under neo-conservative and neoliberal regimes. Words are branded. They are smoothed up. They are polished and packaged in media bites and promotional ads. The name and act of naming first reach the mobs, before the mob reaches its victims. Words are not special, but an attack on words is special because it is an attack on fundamental sensibilities, on the fundamental sites of freedom.

The leaders who practice monologues clearly know that dialogue would lead to their defeat. Therefore, they set up the radio. They design the studio. They plant their spineless anchors in the television rooms. They provide words into their mouths. Like an old poet of feudalism, the anchors sing praises. Criticality loses its way, and uncritical celebrations of culture, society, and traditions become the norm. We have also seen how words are used as labels.

They curtail the wings of words. They reduce their capacities to perform criticality. Mobilized words can create a fear that can be enough to curtail the freedom of individuals and communities. It is very much a part of the culture of curtailment that lynches words in speeches and slogans. It creates an atmosphere of hate stratagems where politics and culture can only be mobilized through hate. The power of a demagogue depends on words. In the world of a demagogue, the word is the first casualty.

Nonetheless, there is still hope. There are still singers. There are still poets. Every time words were overused by pretentious intellectuals, exhausted by the officials, and slayed by the leaders, the poets breathed a new life into them. Every time they felt chained, singers released them through their songs. They have given them new wings to fly. They nurtured them in their songs and sermons. They broke the genres and categories in which words were entrapped. What did Kabir do when court poets were entrapping words by singing the praise of the royal court? He broke genres; he broke grammar; he released words from the texts and the courts. He brought them to the crossroads and the streets to face questions, to face the dialogue.

Words and languages are not innocent. They are products of social relationships. What we need is not the perverts' and reactionaries' attempts to distort their creative potential. Words and languages need to be reinvented and subverted, but not the way demagogues like to do.

3. 'Will You Hate Him, as You Hate me'

Muslim Hating in the Bone of the Nation

Write
Write Down
I am a Miya
My serial number in the NRC is 200543
I have two children
Another is coming
Next summer.
Will you hate him
As you hate me?[1]

Yes, we will hate him as we hate you. We don't have any remorse for hating your children. It doesn't matter whether you belong here or have a birthright. It is no longer about whether you are Bengali Muslims in Assam, or Bihari Muslims in Delhi, or the locals of Mumbai. It doesn't matter if you are Sheikh, Pasmanda, Sufi, or Faqir. It is no longer about good Muslims and bad Muslims; *for us, you are a Miya — a Muslim. And that's enough.* It is ground enough to hate you and take your life and rights. We think that your religion is a threat to the global order. We believe that your presence is inauspicious in this sacred nation. You are a burden that the nation carries on its shoulder in the name of secularism. You are the common enemy of modern civilization. Your beliefs

---

[1] Abdul Kalam Azad, 'Write … I am a Miya', *The Indian Express*, 11 August 2019. Hafiz Ahmed wrote this poem in 2016, in the background of the controversial citizenship acts adopted by the Indian parliament, under the BJP government. After this poem, Miya poetry emerged as a genre among Bengali Muslims to narrate their own stories and reclaim the Miya identity.

are the point of the clash — the core of the clash of civilizations. We can't tolerate you. We can't be friends.

'One who eats beef can't be believed by Hindus' (*'Jo khaay gaay ke gosh, wo na hove Hindu ke dost'*)[2] — my mother, a lower-caste Hindu woman, warns and reminds me against befriending a Muslim person. An upper-caste Hindu cab driver repeated the statement a few years on. He reiterated: *'Dil chir ke bhi de dega to ham viswas nahin karenge'* ('We won't believe them even if they rip apart their hearts for us'). The statement shows the level of hatred and fear ingrained in Hindu majoritarian sentiments.

Habeeb Miya, an auto driver in Bengaluru, remained in jail for years under the Unlawful Activities (Prevention) Act (UAPA), like so, so, so many others.[3] The stringent nature of the law renders it difficult for one held under it to obtain bail. On his release, he asked, '[B]ut why was I in jail?'[4] He got a sadistic smile. The smile expressed the intention without speech, 'Don't you think you being Habeeb was enough?' Himayat Baig was arrested in September 2010 under the charges of conducting the German Bakery blast in Pune. The court acquitted him of all the charges, but he remained in jail. The reason? We can guess. His name: Himayat Baig, a Muslim. The case against Umar Khalid, Ishrat Jahan, Safoora Zargar, Sharjeel Imam, and several others is about their identity.

Hope we remember the Kathua or the Jhabua rape cases — two infamous rape cases in which right-wing Hindus targeted Muslims. Then the incidents of heinous crimes of rapes and lynching shockingly united the Hindus! The plan of Hindutva

---

[2] The literal translation of the phrase would be 'one who eats the meat of cow, can't be a friend of Hindus', but the essence of the phrase goes beyond the friendship context. The translation tries to capture the essence.

[3] In a 2019 amendment, the central government has the power to designate individuals as 'terrorists' without the exercise of due process of law under UAPA. Human rights organizations have cited the misuse of the law to curb dissenting and minority voices in India.

[4] Johnson T.A., '4 Years after Arrest in IISc Attack Case, Tripura Man Freed; No Proof He Helped Key Accused, Says Court,' *Indian Express*, 23 June 2021.

politics is not only to punish Muslims; the point is also to keep mobilizing Hindus who otherwise remain fractured by castes and cultures. They otherwise cannot come out as a group or a community. This is perhaps the fundamental reason for the rising attacks on Muslims by the right-wing Hindu political organizations in contemporary India.

As much as these organizations depend on the Hindu electoral votes, this consolidation based on the politics of contempt remains crucial. In the aftermath of the Jhabua rape incident in the state of Madhya Pradesh, in 1998, the Vishwa Hindu Parishad (World Council of Hindus) leader B.L. Sharma said, 'Rape was the anger of patriotic Hindu youth against the anti-national forces'.[5] His speech did not go unnoticed. The Hindus of the region indeed felt united and mobilized. Time and again, similar situations also arise for other religious minority communities.

The same happened in the Kathua rape case in Jammu and Kashmir. Under the leadership of the BJP, Hindu groups came out on the streets to support the rapists. Beyond rights and moral dilemmas, they mobilized the Hindus who otherwise would still be hesitant to support a rapist. But since it was seen as a rape for the nation, they came together; it was revenge for what the Hindus felt to be the historical crimes committed by the Muslim rulers. All these crimes (from rape to lynching), being political crimes, are also being seen as sacred acts in which lie the security and sacredness of the nation and Hinduism. It was shocking but not surprising that while rallying for the rapist, they shouted '*Bharata mata ki jai*' (Victory to Mother India) and '*Jai Shri Ram*' (Glory to Lord Rama).

Let me say it without hesitation. It is hatred and contempt towards Muslims that unites the Hindu *rashtra* (nation). Hindu India as a nation will fall apart without this perpetual hatred. Ambedkar pointed out the impossibility of caste in forming a

---

[5] 'Hindu Militants Justify Attacks on Nuns', *Agence France-Presse*, 29 September 1998.

federation. He wrote: 'A caste has no feeling that is affiliated to other castes, except when there is a Hindu-Muslim riot'.[6] In other words, it is only in the feeling of hatred and fear that caste societies feel a sense of affiliation. It is only through the act of othering that Hindus can function as a society or as a nation. Since this becomes the foundation of the nation, whichever party comes to power performs this basic task — not only to gain political mileage, but also for the sake of 'national' unity. We have seen often enough how the assaults on Muslims unites the (Hindu) nation and re-energizes nationalism whenever it is in crisis, or feels that it is in crisis.

We know that hatred of Muslims is inherent in the politics of right-wing forces such as the BJP. But how do we see the role of the Congress and regional parties? Here lies the organization of politics around the Brahminical body politic. In fact, the rising attack on Muslims is more about uniting Hindus. This also shows the pitfall of liberal secularists' claim of Hindu–Muslim unity that visualizes an imam smiling with Hindu pundits. The phoney claim of the Ganga–Jamuni *tahzeeb* (culture) rests on obvious fault lines. While the liberals recognize the attack on the Muslims, they don't see another parallel phenomenon — the consolidation of the Hindus. Both are not mutually exclusive processes. They are two sides of the same coin.

This curtailment of the body and rights of minorities in India is not new, but there has been an obvious rise in recent years. It is believed that it all started with the social reform movements in the early twentieth century with the coming of the far-right Hindu organizations such as the Arya Samaj, Hindu Mahasabha, and Rashtriya Swayamsevak Sangh (RSS).[7] It flourished during India's nationalist movement led by the upper castes. It successfully merged language, religion, and nation together through the slogan 'Hindi, Hindu, Hindustan'.

---

[6] B.R. Ambedkar, *BAWS*, Vol. 1, 50.

[7] These organizations have historically played an important role in spreading anti-minority sentiments in India.

Communal ideology was seeded in the very idea of nationalism itself. It was a nation predicated on the upper-caste Brahminical ideology. In this process, both the mainstream social reform movement and the nationalist movement created Muslims as a common enemy. When the concerns are the foundational politics of the nation, the fault does not only lie with right-wing organizations. Despite their secular credentials, Gandhi and Nehru too identified Hinduism with the ideology of nationalism. In his letter to his daughter, Nehru wrote:

> Hinduism became the symbol of nationalism. It was indeed a national religion, with all those deep instincts, racial and cultural, which form the basis everywhere of nationalism today.[8]

What a joke! We are now talking about right-wing hatred towards Nehru, knowing that the hatred towards Nehru and Gandhi is not exactly hatred towards Nehru and Gandhi but towards Muslims. What they hate is their 'appeasement' of Muslims. Their distaste for secularism is equally propelled by their disgust for Muslims.

Curtailment is a Process!

Curtailment is a process that blows slowly like slow wind chips away the surface of a stone. It is slow cooking that begins with the making of the broth. It starts with suspicion; it turns into alienation; it creates an enemy. It culminates in crime and genocide. It does not happen in one day. Even though one might participate in it spontaneously, a riot is not a spontaneous act. It needs planning and execution. It must fuel suspicion; it must spread hate before it spreads. It slowly marks the bodies; it slowly marks the houses; it slowly creates boundaries. It slowly replaces one ecosystem with

---

[8] Jawaharlal Nehru, *The Discovery of India* (New York: John Day Company, 1946), 129.

another. Even if it does not change the DNA, it performs genetic engineering to change the social fabric of a society. We do enter the Hindutva ecosystem. By the time we realize it, hatred enters our hearts. It enters our muscles and bones. It becomes a chilled-out game. The curtailment of others' rights brings sadistic pleasure.

Let me tell you the story of how it entered my home.

Hasni *daiya* (sister) was a vegetable vendor in my village, who died shortly after Prime Minister Modi laid the foundation stone of the Ram temple at Ayodhya in 2020. She would carry vegetable baskets on her head, calling out, '*Sabzi leba he?*' ('Will you buy vegetables?'). Despite her fragile age, she would pull her cart along with her son, much like Bertolt Brecht's Mother Courage going to war every day. I am not sure whether she knew or even cared about whether they were building a temple or pulling down a mosque in Ayodhya. If she heard of communal tension in the village, she would go and hide. She would come out when she felt safe.

When my mother broke the news of her death to me, we both became silent for some time. My mother told me that she was feeling weird that *daiya* was no more and that we would not see her again. The loss could be heard in her broken words. She told me that she did not change at all: 'Hasni *daiya* was same like she was forty years back.' Her image has stuck with me: A smiling, frail, low-caste Muslim woman walking with vegetables on the low-caste Hindu streets. She was selling vegetables when the Babri Mosque was razed. She was selling mangoes when the Mumbai riots happened and the city was ripped apart. She was picking red vegetables when Gujarat was burning red in 2002. She was sitting amidst heaps of onions when Delhi was burning in 2020. In fear, in courage, in the cold, in the rain, in the hot summer, she was out with her basket and cart.

My mother was unhappy when Hasni *daiya*'s granddaughter eloped with a young boy from her caste. Though, as a woman, she didn't have any rights in the male-dominated *panchayat* — an elected village council — she supported the boycott of the family until she was told about the crime of her own son. 'But she is a Hindu', she argued. 'But we don't know whether your son is married to a Hindu or a *Miyani* (Muslim woman)?' Her argument was ripped apart by the other side. And the blame game began. What about her? What about him? What about your son? What about your daughter? Shall I open your mouth about your daughter's in-laws? The village's caste *tola* (ward) soon realized that the rules had been breached in every household. The head of the village, who used to be the moral police, remained silent as his own son married a Muslim woman. The police station did not intervene because it was not a case of alleged love jihad.[9] As shit covered their faces and everyone was exposed, they decided to go together. They all accepted the invitation in the fear that they may also be boycotted for the same reasons. Hasni *daiya* knew these stories of everyone. Whenever someone made jokes about her, she would retort in the same language.

Growing up in my village in Bihar, there were no Hindus or Muslims. There were castes and castes. There were Hindu castes and Muslim castes. Not to hide the fact that Muslims in India have a worse caste system. 'Muslims' would call the so-called Hindus by their caste names, such as Chamar, Dusadh, Gwala, Rajput, and Pandit. It was the same for the lower castes who would call others Sheikh, Bakkho, Jolaha, Rangrez, and so on. Hasni *daiya* was a Kunjraini (a caste of vegetable sellers) before she became Miyani (Muslim). Dildar was of the Beldar (sweet-maker) caste before he became a Hindu to the Muslims. The landmarks changed fast after the mosque fell in Ayodhya. It changed fast when India signed the treaty to open the market. New religion and the new market created a new geography. The communal polarization was at its peak. They were all turning into Hindus or Muslims.

The name of my village is Ushmanpur, after the name of a Muslim, Ushman Miya. The name slowly receded in common

---

[9] An Islamophobic conspiracy theory believes that Muslim men target Hindu women for conversion to Islam by means of love and deception.

usage as Muslims gradually vanished from the village. With the growing ghettoization and the fear of riots, they found their own 'Muslim locality'. Ushmanpur still appears in the land records. An old man from the village read the record and told me, 'Your land and village belong to Ushman Miya.' I asked: 'Who was he?' 'Let's not dig', said he.

My mother fondly remembers her *nana's* (maternal grandfather) friendship with a Muslim man, Kamruddin or Kamru Hasan. When her *nana* was dying, he was holding the hand of Kamru Miya. He asked him to promise that after his death, he would take care of his family members. He would treat his children as his own children. Kamru Miya fulfilled the promise for three generations. The family shared joy and sorrow more than any other family nearby. Whenever the family was in need, Kamru Miya's family stood by before any Hindu family came into the scene. In the situation of the riot, Kamru Miya's family would move into my mother's family as Kamru had a sense of oneness and ownness. The family would hide them under their eyes and skin.

'You have to kill me before Kamru', and the rioters returned when the riot broke out after Partition. As Muslims felt unsafe in the 'Hindu' locality, Kamru Hasan's family, like many other families, moved to Biharshareef, a Muslim locality that is around 80 kilometres from the state's capital of Patna. They still exchange cards during marriages and deaths, but the touch is gone. The emotions evaporated as the physical distance grew. They lost the bond. In the same maternal grandfather's family, when the great-grandson developed a friendship with a Muslim boy, the family raised an uproar. The father tried to convince him; the mother tried to dissuade her son. His grandfather made the same remark, 'One who eats beef, can't be believed by Hindus'. I know he would dare not say this to the family who raised him in difficult days, but what to do with the hate! Despite pressure and discouragement, the great grandson's friendship continues with greater faith. My mother keeps inquiring about Hasni daiya's next generation.

That's hope. Amidst hatred, an emblematic image emerged from Covid-19. That was the photograph of Amrit Kumar dying in the lap of Mohammed Saiyub. It was the affirmation that love, life, and friendship would hold us together.

In Bihar and many parts of north India, we don't use the term *danga* (riots) for Hindu–Muslim clashes. We don't try to hide it. We keep it simple. We say it aloud: *Miyamari* (massacre of Muslims). For many years now, all the riots were *Miyamari*s. This is also true of the present context. Muslims, or for that matter any other minorities, are not in the position to retaliate against the majority.

We, as children and teenagers, would often crack communal jokes on Hasni *daiya*: 'You reduce the price or pay the price, *Miyamari ho jaega*' (massacre of Muslims will happen). She would smile. We would laugh. Baskets and carts would move on. It did not occur to us how these communal jokes might have hurt her sentiment. It hardly mattered to us how her young children were taking those communal jokes. It never mattered to us whether they felt terrified or disgusted with our attitudes. Genocidal words were part of our jokes; fundamentalism was fundamental to our fun.

Hatred in the Bone

Once, a Muslim friend couple invited us for dinner. Though both had turned into atheists, how can you avoid the religion that goes with names. In popular perception, if you are Reyaz, you are Muslim, if you are Prakash, you are Hindu. We carry a divisive colonialism: you are either Hindu or Muslim or Sikh or Christian. Names bring your caste-religious identity together and into the open. The friends offered us delicious mutton *biryani*. My mother loved mutton. She would chew the bone with affection as if she found divine nectar in it. But as soon as she heard that my friends were Muslim, she started looking for excuses not to go. She joined us under pressure. We rushed to eat and started relishing the meat. I realized that my mother was not comfortable. Holding the bone in her hand, she was pretending to eat. She felt as though she would throw up. She was almost going to cry. Disgust was in her eyes. She was getting goosebumps. She could not pretend like the social elite. Her disgust was out in the open. I felt embarrassed. I was fuming. 'What was that? You hate them because they are Muslims'. 'It is not true', she said. There was something seated deep in her psyche. 'I tried hard to convince myself but I was unable to eat. My body was not ready to take it … I was trembling', she said. One day, I was thinking about the incident. My mother was honest. She had a genuine hatred. The hatred towards Muslims had entered her bones and psyche.

My own case was not that different. Coming from a north Indian 'Hindu family', I remember I could not think of eating beef initially. Whenever I would eat beef, the image of my lovely cow and the image of the Muslim would come into my mind. I would have a sense of guilt. I too felt nauseous. The deep-seated prejudices and socialization stand against our rational decision-making. These strong predispositions are deposited under our bones. Though communities have their caste, class, and geographical locations, when it comes to hating Muslims, I can certainly say that if Hindus have a hatred in their bellies for Dalits, they have a hatred in their bones for the Muslims.

I am reminded of my school days in Bihar. To mark our attendance in the classroom, we would say *'Bharat Mata ki jai'* in place of saying present or absent. It used to somehow go like this: 'Roll no. 1', *'Bharat Mata ki jai'*, 'Roll no. 2', *'Vande Maataram'* (Mother, I bow to thee). LOL. In the same vein, most government schools had Hindu prayers. They were prayers to Hindu gods and goddesses, Saraswati, Ganesh, or Antaryami. But this was not a joke when you had Muslim students in class. They would be largely silent. It was working as a silent revolution for the Hindutva mobilization. I asked my Muslim friend, who was my classmate then, how he felt. He said, 'We used to only take it as *tarana* (song).' He smiled, and I did too. How innocent we were. How innocently alienation had already assumed the normal course.

All of us who went to school in the cow belt in north India have written more essays on the cow than love letters! The essay would start with '*Gaay hamari mata hai*' ('The cow is our mother'). Writing was an act of owning. Once you assume that the cow is your mother, the one who eats beef becomes your enemy. Muslims, Christians, and Dalits become your enemy. Subconsciously, the idea seeps into our minds. We would write about how useful the cow is. For example, like a mother, she gives us milk. Her dung and urine are useful for sacred and agricultural purposes. Her bones are used for minerals and her skin is for leather. But we were never told that cows also had meat. It took me years to realize that cows had flesh, meat, and blood too. When I saw goats and chickens, I would immediately see meat; when I saw a cow, I would see milk, urine, and dung, and also the figures of the deities covering the different parts of her body as it was depicted on popular calendars. One day, a Chinese friend told me, 'Dear, don't mind it; it is all meat.' How dumb I was! Wasn't it a fantastic and manipulative erasure?

We were on a field trip in Banaras after Modi became prime minister in 2014. It was the month of Ramzan. Migrant Muslim workers were returning home to celebrate the month with their families. As we were waiting for our bags to arrive on the conveyor belt at the airport, we could see that some bags had Indian flags on them. Some people had badges of the national flag. The so-called Hindus were carrying nothing, no flags, no badges, no marks of nationalism. Their names were enough. They were born nationalists.

After the 1990s, after the demolition of the Babri mosque in Ayodhya, the distinctions were getting sharper every day, with everything being marked. Coconuts symbolized Hindus; walnut, Muslims. Palm was recognised as Muslim; banana as Hindu. The divide was getting sharper. It was dividing at the sacred, sensuous, and sensational levels. Bhajans were fine, but the azaan was ominous to the morning. From boundaries and walls, the divider was reaching a tactile level. Green was of the Muslims, saffron of the Hindus. And it goes on, from the Hindi–Urdu divide to the cultural clash.

During our trip to Banaras, we went to meet a head of the Kabir *math* in Banaras. A fine gentleman told us that he was rescuing Kabir's writings by erasing the terms that have come from the Islamic world — the terms that had Turkish, Persian, or Arabic lineage. The growing estrangements have created strange encounters. In many parts of north India, encountering Muslims is like encountering a stranger. Look! We found a Miya or a Mullah! And the rest of the narrative is set: the person is either planting bombs, skinning or stealing a cow, or luring a Hindu girl to elope. While postcolonial scholars are vocal in their criticism of orientalism, what about *desi* (native) orientalism? Muslims in India are seen to represent all the stereotypes that Edward Said talks about in his seminal work *Orientalism*. Be it Muslim men as lustful and predatory or dangerous terrorists. Shall we call it Orientalists' orientalism or Indian racism?

So, what is it to be Muslim in India? Your house can be marked. Your name can land you in prison; it can agitate somebody; it can deny you fundamental rights; it can get you killed. Once you are recognized as Muslim, you become an extrajudicial subject. A citizen outsider. The name itself becomes a label of treason, so much so that residential colonies in big cities will not lend their houses to Muslims. Muslims are the body and metaphor for the nation's illness today. If breathlessness is the metaphor for curtailment, Muslims in contemporary India are its perfect subjects.

Neither my story nor my mother's stories are special. They are stories of everyday lives, of hope, betrayal, and erasure of Muslim lives in India. My mother might support the rioters in rhetoric after watching Hindi news channels. I am sure that she will still stand with the children of Hasni *daiya*. She will sing the praises of Kamru Miya. She would still bow her head to all the five *pirs* (spiritual gurus); she would still visit a *dargah* (tomb of a Muslim saint) for her spiritual needs. She still says, Miya devtas (folk deities of Muslims) are very powerful, you should visit them. It is not so easy to erase communities from cultures and landscapes. The memory of Kamru Miya dies hard. When my maternal aunt asked her son not to share a room with a Muslim friend, he refused. It is not because he had read some books on social harmony. He did it in defence of friendship. He did not feel it was right. I could have been part of a lynch mob like many others if I would not have been sensitized against hate. Hope against hate is the way out.

The Sacred Contagion

The virus and hate went viral at the outset of Covid-19 in 2020. If we are to believe the Indian government and media, the most dreaded terrorists in India do not carry grenades, rocket launchers, or AK-47s. In place of AK-47s, they carry Covid-19. The Indian media reported that these bioterrorists were equipped with biological weapons imported from Wuhan of Maoist China. The rumour was rife that the Tablighi Jamaat, the organization responsible for a congregation in Delhi in 2020, had implanted viral chips on Muslim bodies that reproduced the contagion to eliminate the Hindus. The new 'terrorists' sputtered the coronavirus in place of exploding grenades.

One part of the attack was that they would spit on vegetables and fruit; they would sneeze from windows so that the virus could spread to Hindu localities; they would cough from their houses, and they would vomit from their burqas as part of these new attacks. They would sprinkle urine on the fruits to infect the purity of Hinduism. These may look bizarre, but this is how the Indian state and media blamed Muslims for spreading the coronavirus.

The violent imagination shows that Islamophobia in India is no longer a closed-minded hatred. Neither is it an open secret. It has been proliferating during the pandemic. From village to town, it was out in the lockdown. It has blown out in the public branding of all Indian Muslims as terrorists — the source of all evil. The perception produces an analogy in which Hindus can be seen as what the sociologist Émile Durkheim terms as a 'sacred contagion'.[10] In the same vein, Muslims can be referred to as the 'dangerous contagion'. Durkheim said that contagion is not a secondary process; rather, it is the very process through which sacredness is acquired and prohibitions are maintained.

While the sacred contagion with the notion of security has every right to spread, we must curtail and contain the 'dangerous contagion'. Since caste remains the model of sanctity in Hinduism, the acts can be seen as an attempt to impose Hindu social order on Muslim communities in which they become 'terrorist' by birth, as one becomes 'Brahmins' and 'Untouchables', or as nomads become born 'criminals' and performing communities become 'prostitutes'. It does not mean that Muslim society does not have a caste system. But they cannot have religious sanctity and scriptures like the Hindus to justify their claims. Their social systems are not yet fully subservient to the model of aggressive Hinduism and its penetrating caste system.

Misapprehended Muslims are a world of chaos for Hindus. They have the potential to produce dangerous contagions. The pandemic came as an opportunity for the state to contain and quarantine Muslims who remained at large, who they could not contain during the anti-citizenship (anti-CAA-NRC) protest. It can also be argued that Muslims as coronavirus is no longer about the illness as a metaphor, as the Chinese are associated with corona or the Spanish with the flu or Hindus with *haiza* (cholera) and meningitis. It is not a case of disease as a metaphor, as Susan Sontag would suggest in a secular society; it is a disease beyond a metaphor. The disease is rather a sign of good and evil that emanates. The evils must be dispelled as a mythic state dispels others' right to citizenship.

An epidemic is never about the epidemic or a disease about

---

[10] Emile Durkheim, *The Elementary Forms of the Religious Life*, translated by Karen E. Fields (New York: Free, 1995), 328.

the disease. Neither the plague nor the Covid-19 pandemic can be viewed in isolation, though isolation is supposed to be the only way out from it. A virus — a microscopic agent — creates its microcosm before it enters the body and society. Albert Camus brings this connection alive in *The Plague.* The classic is about the epidemic, but it is also a metaphoric tale of the Nazis' occupation of the body and the city. It is also about the absurdity of life and death that we face in a time of deep catastrophe. But it is also about the profundity of death that we don't recognize unless we face it.

An epidemic is a moment of turmoil. It lays out a siege in our planned life. It stops our movements and shakes all the structures. It creates a situation in which minor concerns become insignificant. It leads human societies to open in a profound rupture. It is a time when we ask the questions of life and death, of prophecy and philosophy, of encounter and intimacy, about the power of a virus and the collapse of the world order. This should have been ideally the case. Ideally, one would not have thought about communalizing a disease that has become such a huge concern. One can get infected at any moment. At any moment, life could be at risk. One can risk social life at any moment, knowingly or unknowingly. Even if security is sacred in surveillance capitalism, no one can guarantee security in the time of the pandemic. Everyone is vulnerable in the face of the pandemic.

In the moments of helplessness, Camus says, what else we can do but love fellow human beings. He asks us to bring life to the *hospice*, never to the hospital. A meaningful and compassionate life that capitalism and the systems of exploitation have divorced from us.

It is believed that the epidemic erased all forms of social and political differences, but this is not the case. Time and again, the pandemic has proved that politics has no exit, even in death. Who will die and who will survive is not purely a matter of chance; it is a matter of politics too. It has been proven before. It has been proven again with every death of a Black person at the heart of the US Empire and the massive number of deaths of particularly marginalized communities caused by the poor health system. A timely slogan reads like this: *Coronavirus is a disease, capitalism is pandemic.* If this is the case, then it is a right to ask the right questions.

The questions that we have never asked: about our health systems, about the profit order, about the life insurance companies that keep promising us life after death. Let's question the dead health system that forgets the diseased; even doctors are not safe. The virus was there, but we have also seen that it is not the infection that is to be blamed for the deaths. It is the government; it is the system; it is a case of the negligence of the state.

The Scapegoat of the Majority

Writing on the plague, the French critic René Girard said that 'the distinctiveness of the plague is that it ultimately destroys all forms of distinctiveness'.[11] A pandemic could have been a great equalizer. Unfortunately, this was not the case. An epidemic was never the equalizer. It rather brought discrimination, stigmatization, and xenophobic feelings against the perceived enemy. The Jews were stigmatized in Europe during the plague, and the Hindus and Sikhs for plague, cholera, and meningitis in the US Pacific and Canada.[12] Hitler's Germany almost exterminated Gypsies by decreeing the focus on combating the Gypsy Plague.

Srijan Shukla points out how 'the coronavirus pandemic is causing societies to find their own personal scapegoat to blame'.[13]

[11] René Girard, 'The Plague in Literature and Myth', *Texas Studies in Literature and Language* 15, no. 850–833 :(1974) 5.

[12] Anjana Prakash, 'There Was a Time "Fake News" Was Used to Target "Hindus" for Spreading Diseases', *The Wire*, 7 April 2020. https://thewire. in/communalism/there-was-a-time-fake-news-was-used-to-target-hindus-for-spreading-diseases

[13] Srijan Shukla, 'Pakistan's Hazaras to India's Muslims — People Are Finding Covid-19 Scapegoats', *The Print*, 9 April 2020. https://theprint. in/opinion/pov/pakistan-hazaras-indian-muslims-people-covid-19-scapegoats/398581/.

Americans are blaming the immigrant Chinese, the Chinese are blaming the Uyghurs, Pakistan is blaming the Hazara minority, India is blaming the Muslim minorities, and Muslims are blaming the *jahil* (poor and uneducated) Muslims for the spread of the pandemic. The French blamed the Spanish for the Spanish flu. The Spanish called the flu the 'French Flu'. Migrant labourers have been viewed as suspects in the eyes of the state. While the urban cosmopolitans have thrown out their migrants, the upper-caste feudal villages have found novel reasons to shut their villages from the already outcasted migrants. Is it not a riotous game to plan in the time of the pandemic? By blaming Muslims, the Indian state and media shifted the narratives so that the upper classes (who fly and travel abroad) were no longer viewed as carriers of the disease. This narrative shift was consistent with the narratology of the nation and the corporate media.

Muslims as a 'Dangerous Contagion'

We need to think about contagion not only in the physical sense but also in relation to socio-cultural and political life. A contagion comes in various forms, from the plague to fascism. It is not always seen, but there seems to be a simmering connection between the physical and ideological contagion. We don't need to go to Europe now to see the connection. It is in front of us. If the coronavirus is a bodily contagion, Muslims are projected as a dangerous contagion. When both are merged, it creates a ripple effect. While the disease becomes evil, the community becomes diseased. The unfortunate congregation of the Tablighi Jamaat was viewed as a big conspiracy. It was seen as an act of treason and a case of 'Islamic insurrection'. The state invoking the National Security Act (NSA) against the Jamaat members who were victims of the coronavirus is no longer surprising. From Love Jihad to Corona Jihad, Islamophobia has many names and forms. The prevailing situation in India also proves that the term Islamophobia is becoming inadequate. The term is too mild to capture the heightened nature of the violence. The violence almost takes the form of apartheid. The untouchability of the Hindu caste system tries to bring Muslims under its fold after making millions of people permanent untouchables. It is the same logic as ghettoization. This ghettoization is also propelled by what Ghazala Jamil calls 'accumulation by segregation', in which identification moves spatially by ghettoizing Muslim resident colonies.[14] As Hindu society insists on the segregation of the 'Untouchable', now it wants to insist on the permanent segregation of Muslims:

> This is a fundamental feature of untouchability as it is practised by the Hindus. It is not a case of social separation, a mere stoppage of social intercourse for a temporary period. It is a case of territorial segregation and of a cordon sanitaire putting the impure people inside a barbed wire into a sort of cage.[15]

The 'impure' have to be permanently isolated and discarded. Spitting is a new form of attack that is believed to not only spread the disease but also pollute the purity of the Hindu social order. It is the ritual logic of purity and danger. The notion of Muslims as a dangerous contagion cannot be separated from the Hindus as a sacred contagion. As a sacred contagion, Hinduism has the right to spread anywhere and everywhere, from air to earth, from birds and animals to dust. Thus, the one who comes in contact with it becomes pure. First, it purifies everyone from corrupt leaders to the rape accused. It sacrileges everything from economics to the judiciary. Second, the figuration of spit and saliva as anxiety is less about the disease and more about purity. The truth is that even the pandemic could not escape the endemic of the Hindu social order. It has rather consolidated it further. It is important in a society where anxiety from saliva and social distancing has been

---

[14] Ghazala Jamil, *Accumulation by Segregation: Muslim Localities in Delhi* (New Delhi: Oxford University Press, 2017).

[15] B.R. Ambedkar, *The Untouchables* (Delhi: Siddharth Books, [1948] 2008), 37.

the foundation of the social order.

Brahminism and Islamophobia are inseparable. In the Hindu social order, if Dalits are dirt, Muslims are infections. The image of Muslims as infections goes well with the coronavirus and the notion of the divine nation. In the sectarian Hindus' imagination, not everyone is a citizen or capable of being a citizen of the sacred nation. The citizenry rather is, as Modi said, a 'manifestation of God'.[16] Anything that harms or is supposed to infect the citizen must be a manifestation of evil. From its secular notion enshrined in the Indian Constitution, Indian citizenship has become a sacred notion of Hinduism. Democratic institutions, from the legislature to the judiciary, act as if they are epiphanies, the manifestation of the sacred. They talk in the language of religious scriptures.

The sacred contagion of Hinduism holds the centre. It is the mythical archetype by which security assumes the notion of sacredness and illness becomes an affliction of evil forces. It is the premonition of the mythical society that is fighting a divine war against the coronavirus. Muslims are a dangerous contagion not only because they are in contact with danger, but they also have the potential to slow down or cease the spread of the sacred contagion of Hinduism. It operates by the ritual logic of purity and danger. Mary Douglas writes, 'To have been in the margins is to have been in contact with danger, to have been at a source of power'.[17]

The politics was never so obvious as it was during the pandemic. The Indian mission of fighting the coronavirus was not only about containing the virus but also about containing Muslims forever. Both the evils had to be contained in the eyes of the Hindu state for the free flow of the sacred contagion of Brahminism and capitalism. It was not surprising that sedition charges and arrests of Muslim activists were happening parallelly with the war against

<hr>

[16] 'PM Modi's Address to the Nation on Coronavirus: Full Text of His Speech', *Mint*, 3 April 2020, https://www.livemint.com/news/india/pm-modi-s-address-to-the-nation-on-coronavirus-full-text-11585886771546.html

[17] Mary Douglas, *Purity and Danger: An Analysis of Concept of Pollution and Taboo* (London and New York: Routledge, 1966), 179–180.

the pandemic. Also, the anxieties about containing the coronavirus resulted in anger and hatred towards Muslims. Fanatically mobilized people need to be shown how much the state cares for their existence. The formula was clear: if you cannot contain the coronavirus, contain the Muslims — the dreaded social contagion that is far more fitting and profiting than the coronavirus.

Illness as Metaphor

In *Illness as Metaphor*, Susan Sontag writes that nothing is more punitive than to give a disease a meaning.[18] But how do we think about an illness? How do we experience it? How do we describe it when someone asks: what is it? Is it like a bubble or a mosaic in your body, or is it like air or motion? It reminds me of Eula Biss's 'The Pain Scale'.

> 'How do you feel?' the doctor asks, and I cannot accurately answer. 'Does this hurt?' he asks. Again, I'm not sure. 'Do you have more or less pain than the last time I saw you?' Hard to say. I begin to lie to protect my reputation. I try to act certain.[19]

But everyone does not think like Biss. We usually take recourse to words and metaphors to describe our illness. Illness is also used as a metaphor. Both are part of the same figurative thinking. The virulent metaphors of the coronavirus and its violent manifestations have brought Susan Sontag's classic work *Illness as Metaphor* back into the discussion. She draws on a range of works of literature on tuberculosis (TB) and cancer to show how illness as a metaphor can be dangerous. She also interweaves her personal experience onto it. She was a cancer survivor and her father died of TB. Both diseases become the backdrop of her classic work.

Just as an epidemic is seen as an insurrection, we can see the imminent violence that metaphors can engender. But is it all about

18 Susan Sontag, *Illness as Metaphor* (Farrar, Straus and Giroux, 1978), 58.
19 Eula Biss, 'The Pain Scale,' *Seneca Review* 35, no.1 (2005), 5-25.

the metaphors when it comes to illness? What happens when illness becomes a metaphor? When the disease gets a name? When a physical contagion becomes a fictive imagination adding to communal flames? What happens when a virus becomes a figure, and the figure a virus? Certainly, I am not talking about a play of metaphors. I am rather talking about the ploy of the metaphors. It is about deep-seated Islamophobia percolating in the majoritarian Hindu imagination. It indeed matters when a metaphor becomes menacing in its meanings.

Metaphor — a figure of speech that can have a devastating impact on minorities when it takes a vicious turn. Sontag calls upon the need to understand a disease without recourse to metaphor. In her view, the 'lurid metaphors' create a dangerous precedent about the perception and experience of a disease. The metaphors used for the disease are of a 'horrid kind'.[20] She argues how using metaphors for diseases not only deludes us from its scientific approach but also silences and stigmatizes the diseased. She gives an example of pestilence, a metaphor for the *bubonic plague* in medieval Europe. The term 'pestilent' stood for something 'injurious to religion, morals, or public peace'. The plague acquired the moral values of pestilence at a point in time.

Illness as a metaphor is not new. Illness has been a metaphor for bad moral quality. Sontag shows how illness is used as a metaphor to demonize others. If the Gypsy was equated with the plague, the racially mixed were called syphilis, and the Jews were called cancerous. They all were minorities. It is through narratives that a society understands illness and being ill, and the very narratives become problematic, what Sontag would describe as 'the feelings about evil are projected onto disease'. And it is true. We saw how the feelings about the disease were projected onto metaphors when we saw Covid-19 with a Muslim face emerging from the backdrop of 'architectural Islam': from madrassas, mosques, mausoleums, and

---

[20] Susan Sontag, *Illness as Metaphor*, 9.

monuments. The use of such metaphors is indeed very disturbing. But we also use metaphors beyond these problematic meanings. We still use 'corona warriors', 'frontline fighters', and 'saviours' for doctors and nurses. Shall we completely ignore the humane sides of the stories brought by metaphors and narratives that involve hope in time of despair?

Sontag would want so, but her anti-metaphorical approach fails on various grounds. First, it is a case of what Laurence J. Kirmayer calls hyper-rationalism. It 'ignores the significance of bodily felt meaning and minimizes the way in which emotions compel thought, choice, and action'.[21] Second, her argument is based on one-sided readings of metaphors and illness, which are positivistic in nature. Metaphors and narratives were some of the fundamental ways of sharing experiences of enduring illness in many societies and cultures. Against Sontag, one can bring (as medical anthropologists have shown) other sides of the narratives in which metaphors and narratives do not necessarily inflict pain and rather work as a balm. Third, the assumption that metaphor may obscure scientific thinking does not hold. Neither has a metaphorical usage stopped a scientific approach to a disease, nor has a scientific approach curtailed the wings of metaphors. Both have different purposes as myth and history. Sontag also suggests that the naming of an illness should be a scientific description based on the symptoms of the disease.

In 2005, the World Health Organization adopted a 'best practice for naming new disease'. This 'best practice' was taken into account while naming the 2019 novel coronavirus. But even the 'neutral' name created a backlash against minorities. It entails that illness cannot be merely a description; it is a narrative unfolding in our time. It is an event of life; it is a rite of passage. It comes with the curtailment of rights. Sontag's suggestion is radical but

[21] Laurence J. Kirmayer, 'The Body's Insistence on Meaning: Metaphor as Presentation and Representation in Illness Experience', *Medical Anthropology Quarterly*, 6, no. 4. (1992), 323-324.

instrumental. Her solution is ideal but impractical. Can we stop telling stories when we are ill? Can we stop sharing experiences when we are not keeping well? Can we stop making meaning when illness is enduring, and it is a matter of life and death? *Perhaps not.*

Despite my reverence for Sontag and empathetic support for her arguments, I do not see it as a solution. In fact, what Sontag suggests appears to be anti-poetic, anti-narrative, and anti-life in spite of its humanitarian concerns. Metaphors are part of socio-political and cultural thinking. Metaphors may stop, but not the thinking. True, that metaphorical thinking can incite violence. Anti-metaphorical thinking may lessen the scope of violence, but this does not appear to be a solution. Genocidal communities will find the language of genocide, sometimes turning diseases into metaphors, sometimes turning metaphors into diseases, and sometimes creating a new rhetoric of violence. Today they are shouting, 'Corona *jihad se desh bachao* ('Save the nation from Corona jihad'). Tomorrow they will shout that jihad is as contagious as the coronavirus. The point is to think of metaphors that can bring profound rupture without ailing the ill. If words can hurt, words can also heal. The point should be to detoxify the metaphors around illness.

The illness narrative of Bollywood actor Irrfan Khan offers a lesson for us. Should we have asked Irrfan not to tell his narrative of cancer? That would have been too cruel. What he wrote: 'I'm here with you and yet I'm not [...] My body has been gate-crashed by some unwanted guests with whom I am negotiating with right now. Let's see where this conversation goes...'[22] Written beautifully, his metaphors are full of life. His words feel like pearls in the deep sea. His narratives generate a new sensibility towards the illness. Perhaps this is what we need. A narrative is a form of life; it cannot be divorced from experiences. The enduring patients see hope and promise in narrative time. The time that does not hold, dwells

---

[22] 'Irrfan Khan Passes Away: Everything the Actor Said About His Battle with Cancer', *Indian Express*, 30 April 2020.

in the narrative. What Irrfan said meant 'wait for me'. In a social media post, Irrfan quotes Rilke, 'I feel an urge to share with you something. I live my life in widening rings which spread over earth and sky'.[23]

It would be perilous to live and not give the pandemic a meaning. On the contrary, in the time of a pandemic crisis, it is only the profound meanings of life, death, and illness that will hold humanity together.

Muslims as an antithetical subject have shaped the core of Indian ideology and nationalism. This is evident from symbols, slogans, and the ideology of history after the declaration of the nation as a republic. The sacredness of the cow, the slogan of Vande Mataram, and the turn back to the Vedas continue to provide fuel to the fuelling of Hindutva politics. As the core of Indian ideology, Hinduism doesn't get disturbed in practice when ruling and opposition leaders start visiting temples to legitimize their credentials to the core — not to the constitution but to the temple. In other words, if the constitution remains India's secular credentials, Hinduism remains at its core. To remain united as Hindus, it has to perform its task — it has to hate somebody. Today it is with Muslims; tomorrow it can be Christians or Buddhists.

[23] 'Irrfan Khan Passes Away'.

4. Dance of the Migrant Labourers

When Migrants Deviate From the Route

> *Brothers and Sisters!*
> *Now the luxurious building*
> *is ready to move in*
> *You may move out [you may leave now]*
>
> — Gorakh Pandey,
> *Swarg se Vidai* (Adieu from Heaven)[1]

The poem poignantly captures the irony of the lives of migrant labourers. They lay down their bodies to build the cities. They raise the buildings on their heads and shoulders. They connect the city with bridges and highways by hanging between poles and wires. They give it a spectacular presence. With affection, with perfection, with blood and sweat, they make the cities liveable. They make them beautiful — a site to hold, a sight to behold, a site to walk and explore the spaces of freedom. But as soon as the houses are ready to move in, they have to move out. They leave the site as one leaves their babies and hearts behind. This deception of labour does not need a detector. It is open and out there.

Where will they move now? Perhaps, they will move to another site, to another city, to other jobs in other capacities. They may go back to their villages, which they call home. They will tell you that they are not going to come back again. But soon, they will be back as their earned wages finish in days. They will be back as hungry

---

[1] Gorakh Pandey, 'Swarg se Vidai' in *Swarg se Vidai* (Lucknow: Jan Sanskriti Manch, 1989).

homes will run to bite them like hunting dogs. Without money, the poor homes turn into hungry tides. They will be back in the city again, again as outsiders, to keep the city moving.

It is the movement of the workers that move the surplus for the capital. It is the exploitation of cheap migrant labour that is 'crucial for capitalist growth.'[2] Yet the same movement can emerge as a threat once they deviate from the designated route of the capital. What does it mean? It means that migrants do not even own their movements. But what will happen when they own it? What will happen when they start walking back, against the desire of the authority, against the flow of capital, against the performance drive that is driving us to this madness?

The Long March

Let me underline the paradox. This was not the Long March of any communist party to establish the rule of the workers. It was the case of a mass exodus of some of the most precarious labourers in the world. The Indian authorities sudden announcement of lockdown amidst Covid-19 led to an unprecedented crisis for migrant workers. The nation suddenly turned into zones of confinement. Overnight, the migrant labourers across Indian cities were out of work. Soon they were out of their shanties as owners felt that they could not pay their rent. They were out on the streets like *pretas* (spirits of the dead) walking in the daylight and the dead of night. They were out in the open without food, job, and a place to stay. They were stateless and homeless, turning into lesser human beings. As there was nothing to lose, millions of migrants began a long walk under the lockdown.

The authorities announced it again. *Stay safe. Be at home. Install the Aarogya Setu app on your smartphone* — the Ministry of Health and Family Welfare would announce every time you made

---

2 Alpa Shah and Jens Lerche, 'Migration and the invisible economies of care: Production, social reproduction and seasonal migrant labour in India', *Transactions of Institute of British Geographers* 45, no. 4 (2020), 1.

a phone call. Smartphones, smart city, smart people, smart India is the name of the merit we know. It appeared that the authorities lived in Yahooland or Lalaland. They assumed that everyone had a smartphone. Everyone could download apps. Everyone could open a website and register themselves for help. Everyone had a house to lock themselves up in. Everyone had enough food to sustain themselves for months and days. At the height of the pandemic, the authorities gave out a contact number that was out of contact. They would give hospitals names that would not admit patients. They offered support mechanisms that did not support.

While the nation claimed to count millions of 'illegal' immigrants, it failed to count its migrant labourers. The Indian parliament recorded that the Indian government has no data on migrant labourers. Isn't that a paradox? Migrant labourers produce a surplus that can be counted and expended, but they become invisiblized. The excess that cannot be counted. They walked but were not seen in the official records. They died during the pandemic but didn't figure in the official death records. The dead were no one. They belonged nowhere.

When most of us were hiding in our homes, the highways were full of bodies. Labourers were walking, defying the authorities. They were walking for their life, keeping aside their rights and dignity. Who were they? They were the reserved army of capital. They were the Shudras (service providers) of the global caste society. They were the walking carrion of modern civilization. They were the Promethean, the archetypal worker who had no identity without work. As Marx says in the *Communist Manifesto:* '[they are] a class of labourers, who live only so long as they find work, and who find work only so long as their labour increases capital'.[3] Migrant labourers are proletariat in the pure sense of the term — working for survival. But there is also a section among them that remains footloose, desperately looking for work. French philosopher Alain

---

[3] Karl Marx and Friedrich Engels, *Manifesto of the Communist Party* (Moscow: Progress Publishers, 1969), 17.

Badiou calls them 'nomadic proletarians' — the workers who are in the state of proletarian wandering.[4] Migrant labourers in India resemble those nomadic proletarians who are constantly on the move, without a home.

They were again walking but not in a single line, not on the expected route. Disowned by the state, ousted by the employers, knocked down by the landowners, and harassed by the police, these migrants were running out of the cities as one runs for one's life. The local authorities detained them like dreaded criminals and treated them like thieves. They were disinfected with dangerous chemicals and mowed down by trains, trucks, and lorries. With the rising curtailment, it appeared as if a gangster had taken over the democracy. Left with no hope, they walked to their villages in the hope that the villages would not let them die. Once in the villages, they were locked up again as they did not belong to them. The migrant labourers were citizens who had become denizens in days.

While the world feared the pandemic, labourers feared hunger and starvation. Uncertain, thirsty, and tired, they had no option but to walk. They knew the city and its civility. Its casteist and racist civic sense that saw them as dirt. They remain suspicious of the city, and in a moment, they become miscreants. They work in the kitchens, they clean bathrooms, they decorate bedrooms. They babysit, but when it comes to the real test, they become suspects. They are seen as criminals after every crime and thieves after every theft. Facing indignity and allegations, they were walking.

Crawling, crying, hiding, they were walking. The ill and the elderly were limping and walking. Small kids were crying and walking. Blistering their feet in the sun's heat, it appeared as if the workers of the world were walking. *Warning: Nothing is exaggerated here.* It was a mass exodus. Pregnant women were pulling their bodies and walking, and so were the women on their periods. The

---

[4] Alain Badiou, *Migrants and Militants*, translated by Joseph Litvak (Cambridge, Polity Press, 2018), 55.

young who dreamt of a new life in the city were walking while burying and hiding their dreams in their hearts. Their escape was an irony. They came to the cities to find their livelihood. They were running out of the cities to save their lives. They were walking to their homes, where hunger was awaiting them. They were walking out of the confined zones to be welcomed by the feudal caste vigilantes in their villages.

It was Mother's Day the other day. Media was full of fond messages. Shakuntala, a real mother, delivered her baby on the roadside and walked. Her walk transposed the memory of the epic story of *Abhigyan Shakuntalam*. It was the same story and the same question again: How many times will Shakuntala be betrayed? How many times will she be displaced? How many times will she be thrown out of the city? This Shakuntala was lucky. She survived the walk and reached her home with the newborn baby.[5] But Saroj Bai was not that blessed. She decided to walk after her son's death when she could not get any support. Her kid died due to the lack of treatment. Pulling the little empty cart with her son, she walked as Brecht's Mother Courage had walked. There was no Charudatt or Vasantsena from Sudraka's *Mrichchhkatika* to put gold into the cart. The stories from the Indian classics were torn apart.

Humanity was put to a halt, and civilization was put to shame. Jamlo Makdam, a 12-year-old Adivasi girl, died just a few kilometres away from her home. Death track was no longer a metaphor for music. It was the only track left for the workers to walk on. Many walked to death. Death walked into many of their lives. Was it an unfortunate accident, or was it a state-ordered crime? There is nothing to hide. Betrayal would be a mild term for this open bigotry on the part of the nation. It was fascism in its rawest form. It writes off the debts of its favourite corporates

---

5 'Migrant Worker Delivers Baby on Road, Walks Another 150 km to Get Help'. *Outlook*, 13 May 2020. https://www.outlookindia.com/website/story/india-news-migrant-worker-delivers-baby-on-road-walks-another-150-km-to-get-help/352658

and reduces the workers to nothing short of cogs in a slave-run machine.

The pandemic has proven that patterned movements do not hold political significance. They make you less unless some interruption or a reversal occurs. The interruptions possibly change the meaning of the encounter itself, as it happened in the case of the migrant labourers who started walking back like moving *pretas* (spectres). They were carrying eyes on their backs and were walking towards the front. Soon, they became spectres for capital as they danced to an off-the-cuff rhythm. The obliged workers became suspects in the eyes of the neoliberal state, and their much-appreciated movement soon became a threat.

Indian authorities were not concerned about the migrants getting infected. They were not troubled about them returning to their homes. What literally worried the state was the reversal that could emerge as a new potential for politics. A march that could turn into a people's march. They were afraid that they might appear in the spaces of appearance — another name for politics. The fear was that they would gather anytime on the roads and in public places the next time. The situation was alarming because the fear was that they might not follow the warnings. It was a serious case of disobedience. Nothing can be more threatening for the neoliberal orders than the defiance of these surplus armies of labourers.

Workers are supposed to walk in a set pattern, in order. They have to be in an assembly line without the potential of being part of the assembly, which can turn political. Migrant workers walking to their homes were out of that pattern. This is what worried the Indian elites. This is what disturbed the former BJP member of parliament, Balbir Punj. He said, shamelessly:

Fact is migrant labourers behave irresponsibly. ... Why [are] migrants leaving Delhi? For want of money or food? No. Just irresponsible. There is no money/jobs waiting for them back home. It's to utilize their forced '*chhutti*' to catch up with their families or errands back home.[6]

The workers are not supposed to go on '*chhutti*' (holiday). These informal workers are not supposed to be 'irresponsible'. They are not supposed to disobey orders. They are not supposed to force their decisions on the authorities. While the authorities largely saw this crisis in economic terms, for the labourers, the crisis was an existential one (besides economic). They were ready to take any risks to go home. They were ready to risk their lives. We can say that in their extreme vulnerability, they produced a 'dangerous' potential. The decision to gather and go home, come what may, was so extraordinary. It was the birth of a new possibility.

They crossed the line. They walked miles from Delhi to Siwan in Bihar and from Mumbai to Barmer in Rajasthan. When tracked on the roads, they walked on the (railway) tracks. When they realized that all possible borders were barricaded, they decided to swim across rivers.[7] In the dead of night, a migrant worker was heard asking what the depth of the river was. At the end of hope, this is the potential we can talk about. Their utterance brings together a sense of extreme vulnerability but extreme potentialities too. It is both the sense of dejection and daring acts that create this possibility. Of course, many died, many could have died, and many returned wounded. This was a form of urgency from which we can see new politics emerging. Gulzar's poem captures that emergent life:

6 'Migrant workers fleeing Delhi is like "driving without helmets": Balbir Punj's remarks stir controversy', *The Times of India*, 28 March 2020. https://timesofindia.indiatimes.com/india/migrant-workers-fleeing-delhi-is-like-driving-without-helmets-balbir-punjs-remarks-stir-controversy/articleshow/74867320.cms

7 Sandeep Rai, 'Migrants Stuck in Haryana Swim across Yamuna to UP', *The Times of India*, 25 April 2020. https://timesofindia.indiatimes.com/city/meerut/border-roads-sealed-migrants-stuck-in-haryana-swimming-yamuna-to-cross-over-to-up/articleshow/75363432.cms

Come, let's go home — and they set off
they will go to die there — where there is life.[8]

Critics said that this was a man-made disaster with misplaced priorities.[9] Some also said that migrant labourers were never on the list of priorities. Ranabir Samaddar, in his important study, highlights this connection by saying that the state has an over-emphasis on lockdown and an under-emphasis on care.[10] But capitalism too cares. Capitalism has acquired emotional intelligence too. It means it can love, it can cry, it can invest in loving, caring, and crying. It can give you more hugs than your mother. It can give you more touch then your lover. When profit is the aim, care will also sell. The problem is not care but capitalism. Capitalism is so careful in caring that it will not be interested in even killing the children of beggars. It would rather have them crippled than be invested in sentimental capitalism. For capitalists, workers are more profitable living than dead.

A worker cannot be more modest than the figure of Prometheus. The Greek myths credit Prometheus for the creation of humanity from clay. He is the one who stole fire and defied the authorities. He is the one who remains chained to the rock and is punished for his actions. Every day a giant eagle sent by Zeus feeds on his liver. Every day the liver grows back at night. It is this repetition through which capitalism survives. That is: keep ripping apart the liver of the workers. *Pause … gauge … plunge … grate … move.* Let it grow. Keep repeating it like the dance of death.

---

[8] "'They Will Go to Die There, Where There Is Life': Gulzar Pens Poem on the Plight of Migrants; Watch Video', *The Indian Express*, 18 May 2020. https://indianexpress.com/article/lifestyle/art-and-culture/gulzar-poem-migrant-workers-video-6415569/

[9] Christophe Jaffrelot, 'India's Second Wave: A Man-Made Disaster?', *Institut Montaigne*, 27 April 2021. https://www.institutmontaigne.org/en/blog/indias-second-wave-man-made-disaster

[10] Ranabir Samaddar, *A Pandemic and the Politics of Life* (New Delhi: Women Unlimited, 2021), 20-21

Death in the Village

After the initial sense of the grand tragedy ebbed, the image of lakhs of migrant workers returning to the villages brought about a nostalgic turn in the minds of some urban commentators. They were once again seduced by the notion that the Indian village is an enduring space from an ideal past — the last refuge of sanity, order, and values in times of global disarray, a resilient idyll. Some were moved to recall the gram swaraj alternative as envisaged by Gandhi. Some felt it was a reading of values that had exerted its pull on the migrant workers; they had seen through the cities as a morally doomed hell, and their love for the villages seemed infinite on the rebound. The city appeared heartless, the village compassionate. But all that vicarious love sprang in urban hearts without conceding the fact that the Indian village is itself the problem. It is the first of the maladies for migrants, the very reason why they are migrants.

The problem of migrant workers is not to be defined in terms of a choice between the village and the city. It is about a condition in which they are neither part of the village nor part of the city. Privileged migrants can belong anywhere. They can feel equally at home in Sydney, Dubai, and Toronto, and move seamlessly between Gurgaon's Cyber Hub and Koramangala's pubs. They are in 'hometowns' when they come to Patna, Patiala, or Palakkad. Villages are their ancestral lands, but the migrant labourers are literally called *pardesi/bidesi* (those who have gone to other lands and those who have come from other lands) at home and *pardesi* outside. They are outsiders in the village and outsiders in the city.

The usual way of seeing the relationship between migrant workers and the village is in terms of economics. This entails only one part of the problem. Migration is a response to a deeply socio-cultural malady too. The Indian village creates horrendous conditions for people; it impels them to migrate. It makes the lives of women, Dalits, other disempowered castes, and other minority communities an unspeakable hell. It is a graveyard of individual freedom and equality, the deathbed of justice and dignity. It cannot see Dalits wearing a new dress, or slippers, or riding a horse. It cannot take women walking about freely or 'laughing-out-loud'. Ideas and people cannot meet or mix, and new winds cannot blow. It is adverse to love, life, and freedom of the mind. Hierarchies are so entrenched in village life that any possibility of equality becomes impossible.

Thinking about the village is also about which side of the village you are on: east or west, north or south, or in the corner house? Which side of the village is the temple, and which side is the garbage dump? The location of your house is also your social location in the village. Social control is routine and supreme; constraints are the norm, and everything is marked to that end. Castes are marked, communities are marked, and houses and streets are marked. Objects and places are marked — hence, also, mobility. The village is already a quarantine zone. On the social map of the nation, it has to be marked in red. As Ambedkar said, 'It [Indian village] is a case of territorial segregation and of a cordon sanitaire.'[11]

The love of the Indian intellectual for 'the village' is nothing but love for the genealogy of their feudal-savarna caste lineage. Unless you are feudal, you cannot feel proud of the village or its litchi gardens. Can the landless labourer, who slips in the darkness and silence, feel proud? What stories will you tell when you do not have those rolling acres, those ponds, and mango orchards? Pride comes from a sense of possession. Production? No, that is something else. That is what division of labour is for. The lion's pride, pardon the pun, comes from its power to prey upon other lives. For the migrant worker, the city may be cruel and indifferent, but the village is a life sentence that you escape. A life sentence is not a life, and fugitives cannot be nostalgic.

[11] B.R. Ambedkar, *BAWS*, Vol. 7, 266.

Yet, there is still the soil and the language. Yes, I love my village. But if you asked me to live there, I would not unless I am left with no choice. I do not like the city. Nonetheless, if you asked me to leave it, I would not unless I am forced to. This is not a Chinese proverb that the nation can uninstall like an app. It is about the central paradox of life in which a nation of the precariat lives. I am not a migrant labourer who can represent the 'I' of them. I could have been one of them. Once you have been in the village, it lives in your life, in your dreams and subconscious, in your sleep and anxieties, and it is a part of your body — rhythm, language, and map. It follows you like a shadow. It haunts you like a ghost. It lives in your brutal memory and also in the sense of belonging. It rings in your violence, your silence, and your feelings. When you are sad, you cry for it. When you are happy, you sing for it — a land of social distancing but cultural belonging, such as being together but apart. Like a separated lover, it dwells in your eyes and longs in your heart. However, like a jilted lover, it drains your emotions and breaks your confidence when you meet.

The one who migrates never regrets. The regret is that someone is left behind. They are the ones who sing the songs of separation or the migrants sing in their image. They would be happy to leave the village, not have to sing that painful song again. But do they have space in cities?

Death in Migration

In many north Indian languages, the metaphor for death and migration is the same as are the songs and imageries. Both draw their energies from each other; they merge and become mirages of each other. Take the famous Bhojpuri song from north India, '*Chadhte fagun jiara jari gaile re*'. It says, 'The arrival of fagun / burnt my heart / How did my beloved / forget my love? / He went abroad, and didn't return / Neither does he send a message / Does that country not have a cuckoo? / Did the papiha (popularly known as brain fever bird) die here?' Songs such as '*Kaune khotwa mein*' (in which nest do you hide, my beloved bird), '*Kaune nagariya mora saiyanji ke dera*' (in which city has my beloved put his tent), and others echo this prototype. Is it about death or migration? It is about both. Both the migrant and the dead undertake the arduous journey to *pardes* — the unseen, alien land. Take it as fate or fact. For that society, migration is destined like death itself. It is not a pilgrimage that one takes to understand the deep meaning of life but a journey to meet the bare minimum required for life or death.

The journey itself is about a violent separation from loved ones and also dissociation from caste and community chains. To lose identification entails the loss of family and familial identity. Perhaps, that is why migration is equated with death. If life is the name of belonging, death is its severing. What do feudal families do when a girl elopes with someone outside their caste? They declare her dead in the first performative act. They often perform her death ritual to mark this dissociation; she becomes the living dead. Any attempt on her life is seen as a pious act, so the ritual is only a prophecy of the real. The very dissociation marks the potential for love and freedom. For those who risk their lives for love, for the ones who leave home for dignity, it inaugurates a new life. Death is an opening. One has to die to get a new life and to mark a new subjectivity. One migrates to escape everyday deaths.

Some also return to migrate again, strung between caste dynamics in the village and the nature of their job in the city. While on the outside, they all carry strong elements of *bidesia bhav* (alienation), but as soon as they re-enter the quarantine zones of the villages, *jati bhav* (caste feeling) takes over. This does not mean the village is unchanging. Rather, it is disintegrating — sometimes for the good and sometimes for the worse.

Migrant labourers have no permanent locations. They keep looking for locations where they can work and hide. They run to the cities when they face a crisis in the village. They run to the villages when they face a crisis in the cities. For them, villages and cities are the names of two hideouts: one is a den, and the other is a site. They remain trapped in the dens. They can be located at the sites. The site is neither part of sightseeing nor a digital site that circulates. The site for them is merely a piece of ground on which they can put up a tent. The tent keeps moving. Moving hideouts are the permanent addresses of those informal migrant workers.

There are hideouts across villages and cities. They are neither in the cities nor in the villages. They live in the passages. They live in the villages without rights; they live in the cities without facilities. Are these migrant labourers parts of your cities? Will you call Yamunapar, a part of Delhi? Bihari migrant workers who sleep on the railway tracks in the outskirts of Howrah, are they a part of the 'city of joy' — Kolkata? Do Rohingyas belong to the global city of Bengaluru? This also raises pertinent questions about the city — such as seeing the city as an opening or a gateway to the world and not seeing it as a gateway to hell, not seeing it as fortifications.

Resurrection in the Cities

When workers die in the village (in a metaphorical sense), they resurrect in the city, but not in the face of Jesus Christ but as flesh and blood without a face. Torture on their bodies brought about by labour does not make them God. They become less and lesser. They appear as moving machines. They surface as a mass of people lining the cities without making a spectacular presence.

Indian cities have been a major disappointment to them, particularly for the low-caste migrant labourers who come to the city with immense hope. *City as a site of freedom. City as a site of enlightenment.* Indian cities have failed them. Indian cities and villages are not fully delinked. Identities get carried with the social and cultural capital. Indian cities are more welcoming to upper-class migrants who easily make the cities their homes without getting dislocated from the villages.

The relationship between Indian cities and migrant labourers is one of untrustworthiness. In popular songs of migrant labourers, the city appears indifferent. It appears as the in-law's house and not as a home. It is an alien land without any associations except work. Both need each other, but they cannot have emotional bonds. The bond only exists at the work sites where the body and work meet. Contract is the name of the contact. Once the work gets over and the body moves, the contract breaks, and so does the contact. But the relationship is a paradoxical one. On the one hand, the city and the migrant labourers cannot have emotional and social bonds. On the other hand, it is not a professional bond where labourers can ask for minimum wages and rights. Soumyabrata Choudhury remarks that the migrant labourer is not perceived as a worker 'but as a vehicle of services'. They are servants who do not have the freedom to choose.[12] Leave the dissent, they have to work without resentment, showing happy faces even if they are sad.

Despite their problems with the villages, the migrant labourers do not find faith in the city. They see the city as a blood-sucking machine. Yet, it is still better than a village because at least they get paid for the blood, even if the price is less. Villages are better than cities because they give them a sense of community; even the name of the community is caste.

One moves to the city for its openness, for the equality of opportunities, for the availability of 'choices' to exercise freedom. But the caste occupation from the village to the cities continues as there is a straight highway of the caste line that runs from Darbhanga and Dindigul to Delhi and Bengaluru.

For the city, migrant labourers remain outsiders. For the labourers, the city remains for the insiders. The image of selfish cities remains part of the popular gossip and narratives of these migrants. It is not the love for the village but the lack of trust in cities that convinced migrant labourers to leave the cities during the pandemic. They knew very well that the local authorities were never for them. The police were never for them. The state did not care for them. The public health care system was not meant for

---

[12] Soumyabrata Choudhury, *Now It's Come to Distances: Notes on Shaheen Bagh and Coronavirus, Association and Isolation* (Delhi: Navayana, 2020), 107.

them. At least, in the villages, they could still get some money on loan. Maybe on debt, maybe to be returned with great interest. Even that is perhaps not possible in the city. The moral depravity of the city swayed the migrants to leave the cities.

Do work in cities, but do not trust cities. A person can be soft-spoken, but they can suck your blood with love while calling you son, sister, and daughter (*beta-beti kahke khoon chus lega*). The point is that the city lacks the heart to love. It cannot love; it cannot be loved, and thus, it cannot be believed. The perceptions of migrant workers are not without reason.

A city does not recognize workers without work. They are reduced to their working identities. They cannot be individuals; they cannot be a collective; they cannot be a society; they cannot be anybody except workers. As soon as this relationship is defamiliarized, a worker becomes an unrecognized figure. This is true for the workers of the unorganized sectors. It is truer for the migrant workers who often die in their workplace without being called by a proper name their entire life.

While Indian cities open up the possibilities for women and the lower castes, it still remains unsafe for them. If Indian villages are dens, Indian cities are colonies, both in terms of thinking and in relation to spatiality. In my childhood, a friend would proudly tell me his family lived in a colony. I would think that a colony is some paradise where well-off people live. This is very true from the point of view of societal standards. After moving from villages, one would hope that the cities would be different — a space for freedom. But after running from the villages, they get contained in *jhuggis* — a slum dwelling or a *kholi* (chawl) in the city. But what happens when the city mirrors the villages? This is the starkest of ironies that comes into the life of a migrant labourer. Indian cities are turning into villages with their casteist and localized attitudes. To revisit Ambedkar's words: 'What is the village but a sink of localism, a den of ignorance, narrow-mindedness and communalism?'[13] That fits the city today! Look at Delhi, the Jat *gali* (street), Jatav *galis*, the elite residential associations blocking some communities. The Pinjra-tod (Break the Cage) women, freedom in their very name, asked for what cities are supposed to offer — freedom — and for this, they were locked up!

The problem is also related to the question of visibility. The city neither counts nor recognizes migrants as citizens. While their roll call happens daily, they are absent in the government registers. They remain stateless citizens. Migrant workers are everywhere in the cities. Like the slaves of Rome, they are priced and sold in Gurugram. They spread like an umbrella once the traffic stops in Delhi and Bengaluru. They carry your food for Zomato, your utensils for Amazon, your garments in a backpack, you in autos and taxis, serve you tea in dhabas and coffee in restaurants, cook in your kitchen, and clean your bathrooms. In the cities, they are more pervasive than the virus. They are everywhere. We can't imagine a city without migrant labourers but they remain invisible. Samaddar makes this point about them being visible in the economy but absent from policies. He writes:

Migrant workers are visible in the economy, particularly in the logistical economy — road, rail, bridge, and speedway construction; waste processing; creating the necessary infrastructure for the digital economy; ports; delivery of goods and services, etc.[…] s/he is invisible in politics.[14]

Samaddar argues that 'the workers must be found available and ready for work, but must be kept away from the political gaze.'[15] However, their absence and presence are more than just that. Workers are banished from our eyes and minds as soon as the work finishes. They are like a demonetized currency that does

---

13 B.R. Ambedkar, *BAWS*, Vol. 13, 62.

14 Ranabir Samaddar, *A Pandemic and the Politics of Life*, 84.

15 Ranabir Samaddar, *A Pandemic and the Politics of Life*, 85.

not hold value without its utility, and so their names are banished, names that always come with their work and profession.

Unsurprisingly, a person from the washerman caste gets the same caste occupation jobs in Delhi. This continues in corporate and government sectors too, where low-skill jobs are allotted based on the worker's caste. Caste becomes a criterion to judge skills. Of course, in corporate language, they call them experts. In the gig economy, they are the new entrepreneurs carrying their caste legacies. They will still be called by their caste names. And the city-village continuum continues uninterrupted, and corporates, too, become the den of casteism. In villages, they call it the superiority of birth; in the cities, they call it the superiority of merit.

They are known as *sabziwala* (vegetable seller), *rasoiwali* (cook), *paperwala* (one who supplies newspapers), *pocchhawali* (one who sweeps the floor), *doodhwala* (one who supplies milk). Their names are never that important. Though it is not caste-based names like in villages, it is the mirror image of the same.

Casteism continues when it comes to certain professions. They are *nai* (barber), *dhobi* (washermen/women), *mehtar*, and *bhangi* (sanitation workers). The jobs and shop quotas are distributed based on caste. The caste barricades are maintained. Chamars can only get their quota in leather shops. The recent pandemic has shown us how even in an existential crisis, such identities were strictly maintained from charges/surcharges.

In empathy, they become *bhaiya* or *chhotu*. We know their work but not their names. Their work matters, not them. They often die in their workplace without being identified with their names. Ask who died: the one who used to sell tea or the one who used to wash clothes. Anonymity is expected from the city, but not in this way. The practices show an erasure of migrant labourers in our day-to-day lives. It is the erasure of bodies in our imagination. When they walked, we came to know that there were so many workers who used to work in the city.

The humiliation of the labourer cannot be isolated from the

dignity of labour or from the dignity of the workplace: From the names they have been called by, from the bodies they have walked on. It is about how people are made to feel about their labour. How are they paid and rewarded for their jobs? How do the workers remember their workplaces? As horrible, exploitative, disgusting, or patronizing? Do they derive any dignity from their work? What is the social and cultural basis of this thinking that erases the migrant workers from our thinking and imagination? What are the ways in which the workers have been stripped of their appearance and dignity?

Flights for the rich, plight for the poor, subsidies for the rich, sacrifice for the poor, development for the rich, displacement for the poor, and one can draw an endless list. The question that arises is from where does the state get the guts to practice this open untouchability with its own citizens so that it can provide special flights for the upper-class citizens and stop trains and buses for the poor migrants? The state harks back to the existing social and cultural model of caste untouchability in which migrant labourers can be treated in this way. Second, it also comes from the political parties' vested interests in which workers remain outside, both at home as well as at the destination.

It appears that the lives of migrant workers are exceptions to the fundamental rights enshrined in the Indian Constitution. The right to equality, the right to freedom, the right against exploitation all go for a toss when it comes to migrant labourers. As they walk on the track, we know the alternative map of the nation. It is not the echo of Kashmir to Kanyakumari. It is the echo that dies between Mumbai and Katihar and Hyderabad and Hissar. Left by their companies, betrayed by the cities where they worked, and disowned by the state from where they come, they have nowhere to go except what they call home. The city where they built skyscrapers cannot feed them for a few days. Home is the name of the destination. A home that lies in a dream; a home that is devoured by jati-feudalism and capitalism.

What we have seen is that the migrant labourers neither belong to the village nor the city. They remain suspended in movement, such as a pendulum that cannot slide with the weight. As Samaddar has shown, their movement during the pandemic also shows the risks they can take for life.[16] It is only through such movement that they become visible; they become a part of the assemblies that go beyond their assembly lines in factories. It is the daring risk that still provides us hope in their movement.

Movement of the Migrants

Between the village and the city, circularity encircles the life of the migrant labourer. It is not the departure from one place to another or home to the city, but the constant movement that characterizes their precarity in the neoliberal regime. Sandro Mezzadra notes that capitalist valourization and accumulation depend on the tireless movement of capital, commodities, and people.[17] A neoliberal regime expects constant movement and performance (perform or else) from one job to another, from one sector to the other. What should have been named as manipulation of labour is called 'flexibility' in the neoliberal regime.

The market has invented a series of words to gloss over its exploitative nature. Instead of calling the workers ' employees' — who will have some rights, they call them 'partners' or 'stakeholders' who will have responsibilities but not rights. Wage is called 'remuneration'. 'Mobility' is another name for a job crisis. 'Self-employment', 'friendly environment', 'micro-entrepreneurship', markets keep inventing terms to curtail rights. Flexibility and movement are other such words. It is not surprising that the state has been using these terms to hide its failure.

Anusha Kedhar talks about the dance-based notion of

[16] Ranabir Samaddar, *A Pandemic and the Politics of Life*.

[17] Sandra Mezzadra, 'Politics of Struggle in the Time of Pandemic', Verso blog, 17 March 2020. https://www.versobooks.com/blogs/4598-politics-of-struggles-in-the-time-of-pandemic.

flexibility. She sees flexibility both as a tool of labour exploitation and a bodily tactic. In her view, South Asian dancers use bodily tactics to navigate global dance markets.[18] The inherent condition of flexibility is the capacity for movement. The dance movement echoes the condition of the migrant labourers. Though they are not considered skillful like dancers, they are also considered flexible bodies. They are rarely in a position to negotiate. They are rather flexible in ironic ways. Ask these low-paid workers about their job preferences. They will tell you that *'ham kuchh bhi kar sakte hain'* (we can do anything you assign). I can work as a gardener. I can become a security guard. I can do your laundry. I can cook for you. I can clean your shit and iron your shirts. Or I can do all these things together. You have the full flexibility to use us.

Be flexible with bodies and work is a new slogan of the neoliberal market in which the migrant becomes the model of flexibility. In a real sense, it is just the reversal of flexibility that we can see here. Flexibility is about the desperate situation in which migrant labourers are working and seeking jobs. The neoliberal regime does not allow one to stay at one point, at one job, in one position, giving them a deceptive sense of choices and mobility. They are choices without the guarantee of jobs, minimum wages, and safe working conditions.

Kedhar talks about the limits of this flexibility in dance. But, for migrant labourers, flexibility is not about limited choices. It is about the last choice. In such a desperate situation, labourers look for anything: *'Kuchh bhi chahiye'* (any job will do). When the market says *be flexible*, workers say they can do anything, almost begging for jobs. 'Why do you want this job, if you are working?' I asked a low-paid employee who came for an interview. He said that he wanted to learn new skills. He wanted to make a shift. His CV said everything, the poorly paid youth was looking for a durable job. 'New skills' is what he has been taught to say in the job market.

---

[18] Anusha Kedhar, *Flexible Bodies: British South Asian Dancers in an Age of Neoliberalism* (New York: Oxford University Press, 2020).

With so much stress on movement and flexibility, the only figure a migrant labourer can be compared to in neoliberalism is a dancer. Yet, no dancer can hold this precarity of movement at the same level as that of migrant labourers — in the very act of migration from one point to another. Their meaning of life and identities entirely rest on the movement. Their relationship with space and movement is exceptional.

With day and night becoming flat, the so-called body clock becomes a misnomer in the life of a migrant labourer. They have to adjust their own rhythms to fit into new speeds regularly. Or, we can say that workers never have their own time, like the Shudras. They are enslaved in alienated rhythm. Sometimes, they dance to the cyclical rhythms of traditional caste society. At other times, they dance to the linear time of capitalist order. Between the cyclic and the linear, they have become spiral or bipolar, carrying the disorder of the body and time.

It is not from the figure of a dancer or the movement of an army contingent but from the movement of migrant workers and refugees that we may access the choreography of neoliberal capitalism and the curtailment of the body and movement under an authoritarian regime. The movement of migrant labourers exposed this choreography during the pandemic. The movement in the form of undervalued services breeds a colossal profit for capital. They are not only *naukar*s (servants or attendants) who provide services; they are also *chakar*s — one who dances to our tunes, more like a slave who does not have their own time.[19]

Migrant labourers are dancers who cannot hold an independent sense of space and time. They move so much that their movements lose meaningful interactions and potential significations. They are dancers dedicated to capital. There are no religious symbols that can match the power of brands. Behind the success of the market, sensations of brands, and the flexibility of labour lies the hidden

---

[19] The term *chakar* has Turkish and Persian origins that also stands for slave. The term is used for servants in many parts of India.

and hard labour of the migrant labourers who remain invisible like water and smoke from the clouds. Their presence evaporates in the politics of representation and visibility. They have arrived at the city, but they have not arrived at its discourses. They are the political subject of utmost importance, but they have not yet come to the spaces of appearance. They are moving so much that bodies fail to stay in alliance.

Perhaps these workers need a pause. Perhaps they need to walk back, not to their villages or the cities, but to disrupt the mobility of capital for new possibilities, for a new movement, in a new time. To come out of this system, what is needed is temporal sovereignty. That can only happen when workers do not make an expected move as they did/or were forced to take during the pandemic.

5. The Trial of Art

Poets, Artists and the Authoritarian State

> *Yet harmonies waited in*
> *Her stiff throat. New notes*
> *Lay expectant on her*
> *Stilled tongue*
>
> — Maya Angelou, 'The Singer Will Not Sing'[1]

One of the ways to check the status of freedom and rights in any democracy is to observe how much freedom artists and writers enjoy in that state. This analogy acquires more significance when we discuss the curbing of rights and freedom in contemporary India. The figure of poets and artists carries significant weight, for, in Franco "Bifo" Berardi's words, 'it is the only line of escape from suffocation'. He invokes poetry in parallel to finance:

While the sphere of finance is ruled by algorithms that connect fractals of precarious labour, the sphere of life is invaded by flows of chaos that paralyse the social body and stifle breathing into suffocation. There is no political escape from this trap: only poetry, as the excess of semiotic exchange, can reactivate breathing.[2]

Poets and artists are ideal figures who operate at the level

[1] Maya Angelou, 'The Singer Will Not Sing' in *The Complete Poetry* (New York: Random House, 2015), 177–78.
[2] Franco "Bifo" Berardi, *Breathing: Chaos and Poetry*, 10.

of excess and escape boundaries and measurements. I am using poetry here as the embodiment of all arts.

Poets, artists, and intellectuals have been at the receiving end of the rising authoritarian regime. At the expense of the state, the authority has set their parallel ideological armies. They are out there on Twitter and in the streets. They are also among intelligentsia and celebrities. With impunity at its height, they are out of bounds. You open your mouth, they'll be there to shut you up with their bull- or cow-shit. Some are followers, some are paid, some love to silence people, others enjoy violence. In this situation, the mere expression of independent views invites trolling and threats. And if one is critical of the state, then the threat becomes bigger. Scholars, activists and artists are trolled and harassed for expressing their views. Several of them are arrested and put behind bars. Some of them are silenced to the extent that the writer, Perumal Murugan, from Tamil Nadu, declared his own death. In January 2015, he himself announced on his social profile that Perumal Murugan, the writer, was dead. Some of them have been constantly portrayed as anti-nationals and terrorists — a threat to the nation and society. The extreme repression is new; yet it is not so new. Forget the foundations of liberal democracy that create a group of critics for its legitimacy; the antagonism between art and the state is the fundamental one. We need to see the contentious relationship between the principles of the state and the principles of art. In a way, it is the renewed ideal condition in which the ideal state and art came into being. They are in open confrontation. We need to discuss the very constitution of the problem.

In Book III and X of the *The Republic*, Plato states his problems with poets. Poets (and artists) are copycats for him. In his view, they are imitators of the world, and, therefore, they are far from the truth.[3] They lack the moral character to become moral figures

---

[3] Plato, *The Republic*, translated by Benjamin Jowett (London: Oxford University Press, 1908), https://www.gutenberg.org/files/55201/55201-h/55201-h.htm

or models of society. One of the charges that Plato levels against poets is that they corrupt the youth and incite passions. Poets employ the art of loftiness to convince people to perform immoral acts. He argues that a poet must be exiled from the ideal society. There should not be a place for poets and artists in an ideal state.

Plato's dictum appears so far but so real when we encounter the relationship between the poets and the state. But he also advocates for the poet who imitates the speech of a decent person. Such poets would tell stories in accordance with the patterns laid down for the education of soldiers. He supported the poets in the service of the king and the state. Plato was in favour of the didactic use of poetry. Basically, the poets and singers are in the service of the nation and the state. In the foundation of the state, this class-based approach to art exists across cultures and civilizations. In China, Confucianism emphasized cultivating music according to the rites in favour of the state.

The *Natyashastra* and *Dharmashastra* prescribe rules for the high and the low. The *Natyashastra* recommends that artists must not show the loss of the kingdom, the death of the hero, and the siege of a city on the stage. The debates can be read as the foundation of the problem between the poet and the state. The message is clear: the arts and poets must be subservient to the state or else they will face the consequences. They will be imprisoned or exiled. The tradition continues.

Poets as Suspects

From 2018 to 2021, Indian authorities arrested several activists from young to old in what the government termed the Bhima Koregaon Conspiracy case.[4] According to the authorities, it was a conspiracy to kill Prime Minister Modi. Evidence was planted

---

[4] The Bhima Koregaon case dates to 1 January 2018, the day of the bicentenary celebrations of the Bhima Koregaon battle. The state alleged that in the name of organizing the celebration, Maoists were conspiring against the state and planning to kill Prime Minister Modi.

and arrests began. Some were picked up from their homes. Some were called to the police station for enquiry, but did not return home. Some were packed into a van when they were taking a walk, some were picked up from the streets when they had gone to buy medicines. The situation reminded us of the Emergency imposed by the former Indian Prime minister Indira Gandhi. It reminded us of the poem written by activist, Bojja Tharakam,

> You might be carrying
> Milk for the baby,
> Medicines for your mother,
> Rice for dinner —
> You've to leave everything
> On the street.
> In the dark, unseen,
> You're packed into the van
> Why? Where? Who
> No one knows!
> "Arrest, Arrest!"[5]

Arrested persons include poets, writers, academicians, journalists, lawyers, doctors, and artists. With the UAPA, the list is getting longer. All cannot be named and discussed here. For the authorities, they all are conspirators and terrorists in the garb of poets and human right activists. Well, there cannot be a proper name in the time of tyranny, in the time of polarization. They could be only 'terrorists'.

In 2018, the authorities arrested Varavara Rao, an octogenarian Telugu poet, for conspiring to kill Prime Minister Modi under the Bhima Koregaon Case. He had been charged under the Ramnagar Conspiracy Case in 1973 and the Secunderabad Conspiracy Case in 1974 by previous governments. From Indira Gandhi to

---

⁵ Bojja Tharakam, *The River Speaks*, translated from Telugu by Naren Bedide (Hyderabad: The Shared Mirror Publishing House), 4.

Narendra Modi, the poet's crime remains the same; the poet's quest remains the same. The place in prison remains the same; their voices remain the same. The poet incarcerated may be asking the same question again: Shall we stop disturbing the authority? Shall we stop questioning the authority? What dialogue can one have with the demagogue? What tricks can you play with the trickster? Whom will you ask the question that Toni Morrison asked: 'How people cry, how do they sleep, the sound of silence, rhythm of the body [...]'. Poets have so many questions to ask that poetry becomes the inexhaustible whole.

Several writers, activists, and artists were arrested on the same charges. Amidst the rising coronavirus cases, the state also arrested three artists of the Kabir Kala Manch (KKM) in 2020.[6] KKM members Jyoti Jagtap, Ramesh Gaichor, and Sagar Gorkhe were picked up from Pune for singing anti-Modi songs. The progressive socio-cultural group is known for its sharp criticism of government policy and for raising awareness about casteism, patriarchy, communalism, capitalism, and other forms of exploitation. KKM's radical intervention is evident from the fact that the National Investigation Agency of India (NIA) translated several of their songs and scripts to put anti-national charges against the activists.

In a darkly hilarious case, the NIA cited the parody songs of the KKM on Prime Minister Modi to justify the arrest. In the satirical song quoted by the NIA, they make fun of Modi.[7] The satire was twisted and read as a statement by the intelligence agency. The state made it clear that it would not tolerate dissent and criticism beyond a point. They will be curtailed not only by suppressing the voices,

---

[6] The Kabir Kala Manch is a Pune-based cultural group formed by Dalit and human rights activists in 2002 after the Gujarat riots. The group aimed to create rights awareness among marginalized communities.

[7] Sukanya Shantha, 'NIA Cites Kabir Kala Manch's Songs That Parody Modi, BJP to Justify Arrest of Singers', *The Wire*, 14 December 2020, https://thewire.in/rights/nia-kabir-kala-mach-song-parody-modi-bjp-sagar-gorkhe-ramesh-gaichor-arrest.

but also by curtailing lives. The brutal killing of Safdar Hashmi of the Jana Natya Manch (Janam) in 1989, folk singer Belli Lalitha of the Telangana Kala Samithi in 1999, and the murderous attack on the balladeer Gaddar are some of the gruesome reminders of the curtailing of lives. It has not been that long since hired goons killed three rationalists who opposed conservative politics through their literary works. The new was that the state went on curbing dissent in unprecedented ways.

In this new wave of attacks, anyone could become anti-national. Any criticism could become seditious. Any arguments could hurt the sentiments of Hindu majoritarianism. Any toolkit could become a destabilizing machine that threatens the state's sovereignty. One can say that the state ended up 'democratizing' these deadly labels of sedition and anti-nationals, which earlier were reserved only for minorities. In paradoxical ways, perhaps, the allegations and stringent laws became a great leveller that was not only aimed against the poor, Adivasis (indigenous communities), and religious minorities, but also against the members of the middle class. Most of the individuals who were arrested under the Bhima Koregaon case come from civil society.

Let us think of the question in relation to art, poetry, and imagination. Can an authority detain the imagination? Can poetry be killed in prison? It seems that the Indian state believes so. It has been trying to curb the dissenting voices at an extreme level. One would wonder what purpose it served to incarcerate Varavaro Rao and the members of the KKM. While their incarceration directly implicates their songs, poems, and performances, the incarceration of others is also a question of poetry as long as they are in prison for their words, tongues, and dissenting voices. *Tongues are on trial.*

A Poet as a Conspirator

The pandemic brought on by the coronavirus only added to the already grieving situation. It brought an existential crisis both for life and art. Viruses and corpses were no longer metaphors. Though invisible, they were walking in front of us. Bereft of faces and arms, the virus was real. Bereft of bodies and ceremony, the silent corpse was real. Without much noise, the silent cry was real. The numbers of deaths and infections were not the projection of the finance market; though manipulated, they were real.

The pandemic brought a genuine humanitarian crisis. The tragedy was common. The point was to care for each other, what Sandro Mezzadra calls the 'care of the common'. The pandemic was a threat to something essential to 'the common'. It was an opportunity to develop new spaces for solidarity.[8] But the state went naked. It was looking for a scapegoat. The state found two major scapegoats to save its image: Muslims, the external threat; and Maoists, the internal threat. And the curbing started with the shutdown and the lockdown.

It was a time of trials and tribulations for both the state and the poet and artist. Words were on trial. Tongues were on trial. It was a time of naked poetry. At this moment, one could at least say, like the naked poet Digambara: 'I know who the Murderers are / As a poet, as a pretender / I blame Time / for the time being.' One could have claimed: 'What lasts in all languages / as the ultimate sound / isn't OM / but the cry for help.'[9] Perhaps a more soothing one: 'I will keep searching / for the ear / that can hear the truth.' It was the urgency of life, the search for truth, the question of poetry that brought them to prison.

A poet is a creator. But conspirator — difficult to digest. A poet and artist can model and remodel the cosmos. But conspiracy? Hard to believe. Poets can steal words, artists can steal

---

[8] Sandro Mezzadra, 'Politics of Struggles in the Time of Pandemic', Verso blog, 17 March 2020, https://www.versobooks.com/blogs/4598-politics-of-struggles-in-the-time-of-pandemic.

[9] Digambara kavulu (naked poets) was the pen name of the poets in the Telugu region who adopted similar pen names to start a new movement of poetry in Andhra Pradesh.

shows. If poets spy, they fall in love; if artists conspire, they kill themselves. Conspiracy is not the poets' and the artists' business. But the authoritarian regime refused to accept this. The authority's apathy and heartlessness reached a sadistic level. Poets knew this before. 'In what discourse / can we converse / with the heartless,' wrote Varavara Rao on a night in the ninetees before facing the nightmarish might of the state.

Seriously ill and octogenarian poets, cultural activists, and senior intellectuals plotting to kill a prime minister, the plots were too good to be true. One would have loved to believe this conspiracy as a Shakespearean prophecy. But it neither has the potency of that language nor the depth of a prophecy. Such allegations against poets and activists were not only bad humour, but also bad rhetoric. The case against Varavara Rao and others was not only a poor conspiracy plot. It was also a case of poor prophecy in the language of poetry. A poet could have prophesized: *O Dear Leader! You will also fall like all the Great Dictators.* Or else, like the three witches in Shakespeare's *Macbeth*, the poet could have predicted, 'where shall we three meet again / In thunder, lighting or in rain?' That would have been more conspiratorial.

Prophecy is the higher language of conspiracy. Both have two modes of temporality — conspiracy leaps in historical time, and prophecy sleeps in a dream time, only to rise again like the oracle's prediction that Oedipus will kill his father and marry his mother. The state should have charged Varavara Rao for the prophecy that he necessarily and always commits as a poet. But then it would have been difficult to charge him, as prophecies carry what Albert Camus calls 'the impossibility of proof'.[10] In other words, the authority can charge the poet for only one reason, for the impossibility of proof — for leaving no traces of the crime, for producing surplus meanings, for telling so many stories, for asking unanswerable questions. Like children, poets have inexhaustible

---

[10] Albert Camus, *The Rebel* (Harmondsworth: Penguin Books, 1953), 157.

questions to ask and stories to tell. Varavara Rao writes, 'What needs to be said, always remains unsaid'.[11]

The Attack is Indeed *Special*!

So why are the attacks on poets, artists, and writers special and alarming? They are special because the reason(s) behind these arrests are special. The ways in which the state perceives them as a threat are special. The state's harassment of them is special. Wording crime and the evidence of crime against them are special. Barricading them is special because the purpose is not to capture their bodies but to detain words and imagination. There are other reasons too. One that Toni Morrison has pointed out: 'the historical suppression of writers is the earliest harbinger of the steady peeling away of additional rights and liberties that will follow'.[12] And it is being followed.

The figure of the poet and the artist is an ideal of freedom. The poet is a creator as well as a portal — a transporter of memory. His calls carry the ancestral spirits. Like the hunters' instinct for survival drives them to hunt, revolutionary poets strive to take down the state with their haunting words. Remember the song of the balladeer Gaddar from Telangana, '*Ye aag hai, ye aag hai, ye bhukhe pet kee aag hai*' (It's fire / it's fire / it's the fire of the hungry belly). A popular poet from Telangana, also referred to as *prajakavi* (people's poet), he too was arrested and shot by the state. He was firing songs against caste injustices and the state's structural violence. Silencing him was impossible. The state attempted to shoot him down. They pumped bullets into his body. He survived and kept performing with a bullet in his body. For his songs, he had to go underground. He was jailed. But he did not stop singing. He sang again, 'It will not stop, no, it will not':

<hr>

[11] Varavara Rao Poems, Samyukta Poetry, https://www.samyuktapoetry. com/2021/06/24/varavara-rao-2/

[12] Toni Morrison, *Mouth Full of Blood: Essays, Speeches, Meditations* (London: Vintage, 2020), 10–11.

See, the lion of ants has stirred
The hearts of snakes tremble
The wolves have curled their tales
The herds of cows have moved
The tigers have started running.[13]

The attack on poets and artists is an attack on indispensable human capacities. It is an assault on the bodies of sensibilities, on the fundamental idea of freedom, on their rhythm and words. The attack on the poet is an act of invasion of the imagination. It is an attack on the chord that echoes the *naad* (unstuck word).

The figure of the poet represents the urgency of life. The attack on the poet is the very reversal of that urge. Poets are capable of creating new life and giving life to death, as the world witnessed in the case of George Floyd. In the urgency for life, such poets and activists always live in the moment of 'I can't breathe'. With no time to wait for their release, they turn the four walls of the prison into the heartland of resistance. Varavara Rao once wrote from prison:

The moon gets caught in the barbed wire
Over the prison walls
And we, after singing and discoursing,
Lose ourselves in the dreams of revolution.[14]

The four walls of the houses where women are imprisoned, the prison where rebels are imprisoned, and the boundaries where refugees are imprisoned have been the sites of the most beautiful and poignant poems. The poetry on the walls is full of inscriptions. Are we capable of reading them? How does one read or write a poem when those in power try to sacrifice words for their sins? In

---

[13] Vasanth Kannabiran, *My Life is a Song: Gaddar's Anthem for the Revolution* (New Delhi: Speaking Tigers, 2021), 85

[14] N. Venugopal, 'Even prison walls have not been able to stop Varavara Rao from writing,' *The Leaflet*, 17 December 2018. https://theleaflet.in/even-prison-walls-have-not-been-able-to-stop-varavara-rao-from-writing/

the silence of the sound, Rao writes, 'when a weary cloud chokes the voice of justice / no blood flows / no tears rain'.[15] How, then, will the poet write poetry?

Poetry in prison is like a canvas. It can be found in the head crashing against the walls; in the scratches inscribed with nails; in the walls discoloured by tears; in the *bindi* that once was on someone's head, but now shines on the wall like a sun rising from the horizon. This poetry emerges as a ghostly face, haunting like the 'Scream' by Edvard Munch.

Of course, we have *darbari* (state patronized) poets, poet bureaucrats, and poet corporates, the poet who participated in the riots, and the poet who became the prime minister. We have poets who surrendered their words and poets who surrendered their awards. There are poets who have silenced themselves out of fear, and there are poets who have become belligerent trolls. There are poets who reinvent words and reignite life, and there are poets whose words create lynch mobs. But why shall we not talk about the poets, writers, and activists whose life and struggles have been a message for poetry?

It is the utopian but uncompromising principles of poetry that heal civilization from historical wounds. We need to save and defend these poets. Hiding in the caves of Aravali Hills, the poet Vidrohi is still calling, '*Tum mujhe bachao, main tumhara kavi hun*' (You save me, I am your poet).[16] The call is not about the poet's narcissistic life. It is about the urgency of life that a poet senses like a shaman and transports like air.

Look! The poet is in an ambulance entering the emergency ward. Do we understand the meaning of poets in an emergency? Do we feel the meaning of words in a coma? Do we understand the poets, writers, and activists in prison? If we can feel it, it's still fine. If we understand it, we can still withstand, we can still behold the meaning of life and art.

[15] N. Venugopal, 'Even prison walls'.
[16] N. Venugopal, 'Even prison walls'.

When it comes to attacking poets, writers, and activists, then the state has a straight logic. 'They are "Maoists" and "terrorists" in disguise. Instead of doing poetry, they plot to kill the prime minister and parliamentarians. Instead of prudence, they were planning to topple the government!' But one who understands the value of art and poetry knows that this is not the case. The reasons for the attacks emanate from the consciences that keep society sane in challenging times.

Artists as 'Terrorists'

The state's problem with poets and artists is not about individual aberrations; but in their fundamental identities. Poets and writers become figures of terrorism for two reasons. The first is rooted in the questions of truth and justice. 'Truth is trouble', says Toni Morrison, 'it is trouble for the warmonger, the torturer, the corporate thief, the political hack, the corrupt justice system, and for a comatose public'.[17] What they are facing is the problem of speaking truth to power. When they translate the tyranny of power and the irony of the real, they face arrest. When they expose corrupt systems and corporate plundering, they face curtailment. When they give meaning to anger, they become rioters. When they reignite words, their bodies come under the barricades.

The second reason lies in the conflicting relationship between art and the state. It is the ideal relationship that does not go together. They cannot love each other, cannot leave each other, and cannot live together. They will fight, fight, and fight to kill each other, the state for its fiefdom and art for its freedom, and will try to finish each other.

While some of these contradictions are universally true, there are culturally specific contradictions too. Chopping off ears and the trial of tongues is not new to the Brahminical traditions of India. One should feel happy about the improved situation. Forget

---

[17] Morrison, *Mouth Full of Blood*, 9.

poetry, utterance itself was a crime. The Shudras utter a word of the *Vedas* and the king would cut their tongues in twine. But what is new is the idea of democracy and the republic, and if our faith in institutions survives, then the free media and independent judiciary.

To suppress the contradictory relationship between the state and art, the state tries to simplify it by creating an image out of the poet's image. Unlike Plato, who would advocate his problems to the poet, the authoritarian state will not accept them as poets. The state will try to ascribe another image. According to the state, they are 'Urban Naxals', educated and smart with laptops and hash-tags. They can codify the revolution in three words — *Overthrow the state*. They are not like their predecessors who wrote volumes of works. They are their caricatures and lumpens.

While in the state's rhetoric, they are attacked for their incapacity to be poets and intellectuals; on the other hand, the one who keeps the book is also blamed. The one who engages in intellectual work is also blamed. 'Why does he have so many books in his house, particularly on Marx and Mao', a police officer complained to the family of Varavara Rao. This is the paradox through which the state and media presented Anand Teltumbde, Sudha Bharadwaj, Sudhir Dhawale, Varavara Rao, and others who are known as the BK-11 (after Bhima Koregaon). Now it is BK-12. Any day it can become BK-47 or AK-47, de-historicizing the distance between the historical memorial of Bhima Koregaon and the war history of the lethal weapon — the Avtomat Kalashnikova. The attempt is to criminalize the formation of possible assembly in Bhima Koregaon as they did in Amritsar with Operation Blue Star and in Bastar with Operation Green Hunt.

If we believe the statist rumour, then Father Stan Swamy could have planted the terror message in his preaching. Varavara Rao can codify the Maoist's message in his poems. Shoma Choudhury and Sudha Bharadwaj can hide the message in their stories. At his fingertips, Rona Wilson can encrypt the message on chips. Anand

Teltumbde can encode them in the language of management for a global enterprise of Maoism. From that standard, they all are poets and conspirators. They all are masterminds. Or we can say that it is the era of the poet-mastermind. These people can transgress boundaries; they can reignite words. They can reinvent politics. They can visualize emancipation. They fight against the fascists. One of the allegations against the activists says that 'they were forming an anti-fascist front'.[18] The other was arrested for forming an anti-Brahminical front. That is so dangerous. The powers that be are so drunk that you don't need to say that the state is fascist. It claims it is. The state says that they use poetry to disguise their politics. They use politics to 'indoctrinate' young minds, unlike the media, which hacks the mind.

Urban Naxals are blamed for their plainclothes activism. They are poets without poems and Maoists without uniforms. Like the state's Special Task Force, they are the Maoists' plainclothes. Terrorism is the fetish that the state and media have created in the name of narratives. The narratives sell like sex and immerse like murder thrillers. It is what Anne Applebaum says is 'the seductive lure of authoritarianism'.[19] The media works as a manager. With the state and police support, it manufactures lies and conspiracies that work as fuel for right-wing politics. The worst is that they make people believe in those conspiracies. The ordinary people believe that the nation and the leaders are under attack. That religion and tradition are under attack. They change the whole atmosphere into an atmosphere of hatred, fear, and despair. Poetry fails to reignite the senses.

A cab driver in Delhi shows me a picture of Sudha Bharadwaj. He tells me that she is the one who was planning to garland

---

[18] Deeptiman Tiwary, 'Chargesheet in Elgar Parishad Case: CPI Maoist Documents, Letters on "Anti-Fascist Front" Cited by NIA', *The Indian Express*, 15 October 2020.

[19] Anne Applebaum, *Twilight of Democracy: The Seductive Lure of Authoritarianism* (New York: Doubleday, 2020).

Modi in Rajiv Gandhi style.[20] 'But, you know, she does not look like a Maoist, but who knows what is right', he said. *What a disappointment*, I felt. Mourn the anchors! Feel pity for the popular media, Bollywood, and reality shows!

Maoists not appearing like Maoists and a terrorist not looking like a terrorist is not only a major concern for the intelligence agencies but also for the viewers who consume the violence in the name of such shows. Looking like a Maoist, seen as a terrorist, and appearing like an expert is the core of news-making. It is about image-making, it is about belief-making, it is about consent-making. It is about taking people's trust for a ride in the perceptual economy of the appearance by which one becomes a 'nationalist' and the other, a 'terrorist'.

It is not surprising that to make a person look like a Maoist, police and paramilitary forces in central India allegedly carry Maoist uniforms along with their arms before shooting the activists down in 'encounters'. Finding four feet of a body wearing six feet of the uniform, freshly pressed, newly bought, is not uncommon. Like Covid-19 PPE kits, the state's developmental kit for Adivasis is: uniform and coffin together, same size for everyone, from young to old, and gender-neutral.

But such uniformity makes the task difficult for the state regarding the Urban Naxals. The uniform is not enough; the added presentation is necessary. The state fakes stories like a bonanza sale — ten lakhs on his head and five lakhs on her dead body, fifty thousand for any clue whoever fits the red, green, and blue.

Nobody knows who the Urban Naxals are. One who is blamed is not to be believed; one who claims is not the one. The playwright Girish Karnad's placard read, 'Me too Urban Naxal'. But we know that it is not true. It is a flaw, it is a flout, it is a ploy, it is a plot, it is a case of witch-hunting. It is about the suppression of dissenters. It is about the relationship between the figure of the poet and the

---

[20] Former prime minister of India, Rajiv Gandhi, was killed by a suicide bomber when she detonated an RDX explosive belt.

state's authority. It is more crucial when the poet is a pure rebel and the state is a puritanical authoritarian.

The Poet *versus* the State

The meaning of poets in prison is less about the poet and more about the particular state and society. It is about the deteriorating health of democracy and the curtailment of breathing spaces. The news reported that the poet Varavarao Rao was in delirium. It is not the poet who is delirious; it is democracy that is delirious, failing to recognize its self and its conscience.

The poets' fight is not against any prime minister or the heads of state. Their fight is against the moral authority of the state. The poet can ask the state, 'Who are you to rule over my body? Who are you to control my imagination? Dear Authority! Who gave you this consent? Who gave you this right to infringe on my freedom if I have not?'

It should not surprise us that whoever comes to power becomes the immediate enemy of poets and artists. The poet is not only a conscientious objector, but also a perpetual objector. In the eyes of the state, they are permanent trouble-makers who, even for their *ishq* (love), will not let the authorities sleep at night. They have to be exiled. They have to be imprisoned for the success of authoritarianism.

The second problem for the state is that poets cannot accept the power of morality and the certainty of truth. For the poets, morality is a point of departure and love is a truth criterion in a journey that never ends. While the state wants to define everything, for poets and artists, nothing is fixed. It is not surprising that Plato wanted to banish poets from the Republic. It is unsurprising that Varavara Rao was imprisoned by political regimes of all colours, from Indira Gandhi to N.T. Rama Rao. His arrest under the BJP regime only confirms the commandment and reaffirms the poetic commitment. It is not surprising that the artists of Maharashtra's KKM were creating trouble for Congress Home

Minister P. Chidambaram. And they are equally despised by the BJP government.

The Kenyan writer Ngugi wa Thiong'o, whose many works Varavaro Rao has translated in prison, underlines this contradiction: A state is 'conservative by its very nature as a State. It wants things as they are.'[21] He underlines that art is revolutionary by its very nature as art. It is always revising itself.' The state is a state of permanency, but the permanency of art is motion and movement. Thiong'o says that 'the State in a class society is an instrument of control'. The state strives to achieve 'the perfection of the form of things, such as the legal system'.'

But like a black crow sitting on the rooftop of the court and roving over the heads of judges, art wants to test the limits of the legal and institutionalized system, cawing louder than the executive draped in black robes. It tries to test the limits of the system. It wants to see the end of the structure.

The poet and the state are in a ceaseless fight. They fight like a snake and a mongoose, with neck and noose, with words and bullets, with bodies and spectacles on penpoints and gun-points. It can be said that the relationship between art and the state is a case of ontological antagonism. The artist's fight against the state is not necessarily because of their beliefs in politics, but because of the principles of art that are at war with the state. They take an interest in politics because of the poetic and artistic calling and not necessarily because of the 'obvious' politics. Though both are not so distinct, it is important to mark this distinction when the state and society allege that they are not poets and artists, but political activists. It is to make it clear that poets have principled reasons to be in politics and not necessarily because of political concerns.

One figure of such a poet and artist is Pyotr Pavlensky, a Russian-born artist who protested against President Putin. In protest, he set ablaze the doors of the Lubyanka Building, the

---

[21] Ngugi wa Thiong'o, *Penpoints, Gunpoints, and Dreams: Towards a Critical Theory of the Arts and the State in Africa* (Clarendon Press, 1998), 5.

headquarters of the Russian Security Service. But when he was given asylum in France, he set ablaze a branch of a federal bank of France based in the Place de la Bastille. He declared that the bank was a symbol of modern-day tyranny.

Many times, poets and artists who participated in the revolution also participated in the counter-revolution. They again positioned themselves against the authorities' power and the state's permanency. They can be termed terrorists for their disgust towards the idea of the state. But there is another reason they can be considered terrorists. Pavlensky says, 'if there is a scale of expression, with opera at one and terrorism at the other', then 'political art is closer on the scale to terrorism than to opera.'[22]

Against 'state terrorism', the poet's performative act is what Camus designates as 'rational terror'. It is nothing but pure claims against the state that 'we are not afraid of your authority'.[23] The revolutionary poet and artist's role is to change a culture's inner life. As the novelist Bill Gray says, artistic imagination can make raids on the human consciousness.[24] The poet's imagination is about the rejection of everyday life. Does it mean that poets and artists are fundamentally anarchists? True, to an extent, but not always true. As the state wants poets to be banished, the poets want the state to wither away. The act of withering away of the state is not necessarily anarchism. It can be a condition of a high stage of corporatism or the highest stage of communism. In the first case, the actors are corporates or *bhakts* (strong followers); in the second case, they are 'revolutionaries' or 'terrorists'.

The tag of the terrorist is about time. Portraits of national heroes that are hung in the parliament were terrorists at a point

<hr>

22 Fernanda Eberstadt, 'The Dangerous Art of Pyotr Pavlensky', *New York Times*, 11 July 2019, https://www.nytimes.com/2019/07/11/magazine/pyotr-pavlensky-art.html

23 Camus, *The Rebel*, 157.

24 Leonard Wilcox, 'Terrorism and Art: Don DeLillo's "Mao II" and Jean Baudrillard's "The Spirit of Terrorism". *Mosaic: A journal for the interdisciplinary study of literature* (2006): 89-105.

in time. A true poet would refuse to be hung as a portrait in the parliament because they cannot be captured by time. Their words at any time resonate against the state power. Ask the regime, would they prefer to have the portraits of Rahat Indori or Namdev Dhasal? As Indori says: 'Here is a power who can give you a prize / There is a poet / Sufi who can refuse it.' The poet also remains most unpredictable.

Death of an Author

In 2015, a writer in India declared his own death by saying that the author is dead. It was not about the death of the author that the French literary critic, Roland Barthes, talked. Barthes declared that an author's intention and biographical facts should hold no special weight in new interpretations of a literary work.[25] But here, the case was different. The point here was not literary; it was the death of an author in a more literal sense.

'Perumal Murugan the writer is dead. As he is no God, he is not going to resurrect himself. He also has no faith in rebirth. An ordinary teacher, he will live as P. Murugan. Leave him alone', the Tamil writer Murugan posted on his Facebook account in January 2015 when he was forced to withdraw his novel *Madhorubhagan* (translated as *One Part Woman*). In any authoritarian regime, the first sign of curtailment comes with the curbing of artists, writers, and intellectuals. The ascendant political right was ensuring that no literature existed except praises. T. M. Krishna rightly says that Perumal Murugan symbolizes 'freedom of speech but also a marker on how a writer can be broken when his "life's breath" is maligned and mutilated'.[26]

While Dalits, minorities, Adivasis, and Kashmiris were already under attack, the state came up with the new coinage of 'Urban

---

[25] Roland Barthes, *Image, Music, Text* (London: Fontana Press, 1977), 142-148.
[26] T.M. Krishna, 'How I Failed Perumal Murugan', *The Economic Times*, 24 January 2015, https://economictimes.indiatimes.com/blogs/et-commentary/how-i-failed-perumal-murugan/

Naxals' who live in cities and support anti-national activities. They send a call to arms, and all the marginalized sections of the nation take arms and jump into the battle with the state. The corporate Indian media constantly presents them as masterminds and instigators. And the poets' and artists' images go along with the label. Indeed, they are the instigators, not of mobs but of consciences. Wish we could have many poets such as Varavara Rao and artists' collectives such as KKM who enrage our consciences.

The right-wing and consumer culture also gives birth to anti-intellectual tendencies. There has been an attempt to demonize the intellectual environment. From the demotion of the humanities to the lowering status of human rights. While the state was trying to curb dissent in all possible ways, dissent, the free bird, got a new wing. Dissent saw the participation of the youth and the minorities. Dissent led to a bitter conflict between the state and the artists, activists, and writers, which we are in.

6. March of the Mustard

Protest, Dissent, and the Curbing of Rights

> *To protest is to refuse being reduced to zero and enforced silence. Therefore, at the very moment, a protest is made, if it is made, there is a small victory.*
>
> — John Berger[1]

As authoritarianism rises, it becomes intolerant of any form of dissent. It doesn't like criticism. It axes oppositions. It tries to bring everyone into a zone of enforced silence. It perceives criticism as a criminal act, and dissensus as an act of sedition. It takes silence as surrender and acceptance. It criminalizes the very right to protest. The elected leader believes that he will dissolve the people and elect another, like in Bertolt Brecht's satirical poem 'The Solution':

After the uprising of the 17th June
The Secretary of the Writers Union
Had leaflets distributed in the Stalinallee
Stating that the people
Had forfeited the confidence of the government
And could win it back only
By redoubled efforts. Would it not be easier
In that case for the government
To dissolve the people
And elect another?[2]

---

[1] John Berger, *Bento's Sketchbook* (New York: Pantheon Books, 2011), 113.

[2] Bertolt Brecht, 'The Solution', https://www.poemhunter.com/poem/the-solution/

This majoritarianism , combined with the fear and temptation for power, makes the state deny any form of criticism. The insecurity of the authoritarian regimes comes from two sources. First, such regimes live in a perpetual sense of risk and crisis. Yet, they must prove they are omnipotent. No doubt they perceive the crisis; they feel the threat; they feel it more than any other regime. However, they are always in a mood of avowal. But this is only one strategy. They can also adopt a second strategy in which they tend to declare that the crisis is more than what it is. Even if they know the issue is small, they make a spectacle out of it, if it goes in its favour.

Every sign becomes a source of suspicion. The state reads any red sign as a risk — from the book with a red cover to the red roses in a garden. It smells beef in all meats and conspiracy in all meetings. It behaves like the black magician who thinks that cats meowing could be a conspiratorial act. It spreads its tentacles like the Pegasus spyware on all possible forms to sense and censure the dissenting voices. It imposes its panoptical vision on all possible fronts — from food, festivals, media, culture, and education. It wants to know before one can protest. It plans pretexts before anything is planned. It knows the demography of the dissenters. It keeps lurking into the camera. Surveillance becomes its obsession, and curbing becomes a form of incessant campaign. Surveillance becomes the primary engagement of sovereign power. Its media carries the same campaign with fear and hatred, with persistent demonization, with the harvest of shame.

But, these are the dominant manifestations of the curtailment the authoritarian state engages in. They are at least visible. The regime also cultivates hegemonic cultural practices to contain dissent and takes the consent of the popular masses. They do it through the media, education, the judiciary, and advocacy. They create new habits and behaviours. They produce new rituals and festivals. They create a media that manufactures consent. They try all possible ways to inhabit our habitus. They try to implicate their monologic culture into all spheres of culture — from banking models of education to bites from the news media.

Their hegemonic sign does not remain outside for a long time. They ship into our attitudes and behaviours. We assimilate these constraints while walking, during security check-ups, and in our talks and discussions. Fearing the virus, we sanitize our own behaviours. We have seen how the police choreograph our movements during every protest, and we march as we are marching against policing. We march as we have fixed our destination on land that is outside the capitalist system. Curtailment has become a part of our everyday life. While we are not allowed to enter into national zones for security reasons, we also accept it as the norm. The authority reaches the body. It becomes a part of our assembly. We start speaking in its tongue. It is in this environment that even a protest becomes the method of the police.

There is no denying that the ideology of barricading has been shaping our ways of seeing. One day, it was walking with us, constantly interfering with our movements. It was reversing everything that society had achieved after a long struggle, including various rights and access to institutions. Then, the authority and its ideology came to distances.

Everyone was a dangerous subject. A distance had to be maintained. The distance was not only spatial and durational, but also about reformulating the very axis of distance. It was not the assumed distance where two and two could become four. In this new regimentation, two and two could be infinite, more than six as a level. Six feet is not the size of the body, but the new minimum and lower limit that has to be maintained — both in its distance and after death in a graveyard. It is not about size; it is about laying siege on the body and imagination. It is about the bodies on the barricades!

Prime Minister Modi's evocation of the *lakshman rekha* (a line not to be crossed) clearly stated a threshold that one cannot cross — not just physically but also morally and imaginatively. *Samajik doori ka samman karein* (respect the social distance) became a new reiteration of old rules. The language was of sanction, ritually coloured and morally coded. It was against the idea of assembly. It was against the encounter with others — strangers.

Overall, it was about maintaining a distance from whatever can be contagious. Even while one is resisting these changes at the level of thought, what one realizes is that bodies have been so accommodative to these biopolitical changes that we surreptitiously accept everything that we resist. Daniele Lorenzini points out that 'instead of worrying about the increase of surveillance mechanisms and indiscriminate control under a new "state of exception", one needs to worry about the fact that we already are docile, obedient biopolitical subjects'.[3]

Yet, a protest happened. Then also, people dissented. When the majority maintained silence, the minority protested. It reaffirmed that whenever it becomes a matter of life and death, people come out. They will come out. Their coming out itself becomes a statement. Some daring protests happened under the regime of control. Many, many more took place. Protests full of newness — unparalleled in their courage, unparalleled in their strategies, unparalleled in their participation, and unparalleled in their sacrifices.

When people hid in their homes for fear of the virus, the Black Lives Matter protests unfolded in the United States in 2020. When Muslims were at the receiving end of state-sponsored violence, the anti-CAA protestors created Shaheen Baghs across India.[4] When we were thinking about the end of protest culture, farmers marched from Indian Punjab to secure their Minimum Support Price (MSP). The Una protests of Gujarat almost laid siege to the incessant march of the upper-caste Hindus.

---

[3] Daniele Lorenzini, 'Biopolitics in the Time of Coronavirus', *Critical Inquiry*, 2 April 2020.

[4] The Shaheen Bagh protest emerged as one of the most popular protests in recent times. The Shaheen Bagh sit-in is often referred to by the supporters of the protest as a site of modern-day satyagraha.

Despite threats and warnings, dissents were recorded, and protests were made. Yes, the state curbed them brutally. Yes, protestors were harassed, incarcerated, and demonized in the public media. Many of them still remain in prison. But all this also showed that protest and dissent could not be fully suppressed. Some protests partially failed, and some failed totally. Does it mean that they have failed? They may have failed to achieve their aims. Yet, they had already achieved something by making a protest. Once a protest is made, a victory is made. A resistance is registered. A memory is inscribed. Protests do not necessarily end in success; everything lies in the process. It lies in the very affirmation of 'I protest'.

If a Protest Is Made!

If India saw one of the most authoritarian regimes lay siege to the body of the republic in recent years, it also saw some of the most remarkable protests erupting on the streets. They were all unique in their own ways. If Dalit and Muslim protests were spontaneous, farmers came well-prepared for a long battle. The most popular protests were not led by mainstream parties but by the minorities and those on the margins of society. This is crucial to understanding the nature of protests and their curbing by the state and authorities.

Modi's rise looked unshakable after his massive victory in the 2014 Indian general election. He silenced his critics with his slogans in a style that was hyper-visible. His cult of supporters chanted 'Modi, Modi' from Mumbai in India to Madison Square in the United States. His hold on power at the time was so strong that it looked unshakable. It was looking impossible to hold a protest against his regime. One could have been lynched if one spoke against him, criticized his policies, or wrote a critical social media post. You write and you will be trolled. You protest and you will be thrashed.

Student protestors fired the first salvo against the Modi regime in the aftermath of Rohith Vemula's death in 2016. The Una protest in Gujarat that erupted after the flogging of Dalit youths was another protest that shook the regime to the core. It was not only unique in style; it was also forceful in its demand.[5] Subsequently, Muslims led an unprecedented mass protest against the Citizenship Bill, popularly known as the anti-CAA-NRC protests, in 2019. Farmers led the third major protest from the state of Punjab against the new farm bills. Of course, in the thick of the forest, Adivasis led many such protests that remain out of sight in a regime of hypervisibility. Students worked as opposition in the absence of a strong, morally sound opposition party.

Whatever happened to those protests, they shattered the myth and aura of the Modi regime. They demystified a figure who wanted to be sacrosanct forever — without critics, without criticisms. One of the noticeable points is that all these protests occurred at a time when protesting looked impossible. Muslim protestors created Shaheen Bagh across the country when they felt vulnerable after incidents of lynching and allegations of anti-nationalism. By participating in these protests, they did not only serve their concerns. They also strengthened democratic rights. These protests came as a breath of fresh air amidst the scenes of breathlessness perpetrated by the regime of control.

The state used all possible apparatuses to suppress these protests. It organized a mob attack at the heart of the capital to curb the Muslim protestors. It attempted to cut the flowers of Shaheen Bagh. It cut the water and electricity supplies at the protest sites. It tried to silence the farmers when they organized a parallel parade against the state in January 2021. It brutally attacked and implemented stringent laws and acts against Dalit protestors after the Bharat Bandh protest in April 2018.[6] It ran an intense media

---

[5] The then chief minister of Gujarat, Anandiben Patel, had to resign after the Una protest in 2016.

[6] Major Dalit organizations called for a Bharat Bandh (All India Strike)

campaign to break their unity and demoralize them. It tried in all possible ways to criminalize dissent. On occasions, it curtailed the spaces of protests across the state in the name of maintaining peace and security.

Of course, peaceful protestors waited for their demands to be met. They waited long. Some of them dispersed after a prolonged wait. They juggled, struggled, and failed. They also committed tactical mistakes. These mishaps are expected during mass protests. But the failure also occurred because the communities of protestors failed to come together. When it was about the diluting of the SC/ST Act, only Dalits came out. Despite forms of transverse solidarities, the movements saw limited widespread mobilization. When it was about the anti-CAA-NRC protest, it was only the Muslims who were out. During the farmers' protest, it was largely Sikhs from Punjab and Jats from Haryana and Western Uttar Pradesh. The protests led by the *safai karmacharis* (sanitation workers) in Delhi, more or less, saw no support from the outside.

The single irony was that the authority singled out protestors' voices. The state and media kept targeting them one by one saying that they are not farmers but they are a few Jats and Sikhs. When it comes to students, it is only students. Should we say that they all have failed in one way or the other? Shall we say that under the authoritarian regime, protests fail to deliver? Many protests could not register their visibility. What about mass Adivasis protests? In the absence of visibility, do protests serve any purpose?

At this point, one may like to ask, as Zeynep Tufekci asks, 'do protests even work?' His answer is yes. Protests do work, but usually not in the way and time frame that many would think. He says that protests sometimes look like failures in the short term. However, they may have long-term effects on both the protesters

---

on 2 April 2018, when the Indian apex court diluted the provision of the Scheduled Caste and Schedule Tribe (Prevention of Atrocities) Act, 1989. The act works as a deterrent provision against discrimination, atrocities, and hate crimes.

themselves and the rest of society.[7] He says that collective action and participation can be a life-changing experience for many. To be in a sea of people demanding positive social change is empowering and exhilarating.

Protests work because they sustain movements over the long term as participants bond during collective action. It must have been easy for the authorities to curtail Shaheen Bagh by hyping the fear of the coronavirus. Yet, it will be difficult to erase the memory of the participants. It will be difficult to obliterate the experience of the women who came out from their domestic spaces. Can the children who learnt lessons of citizenship forget those memories? Can those children forget the lesson of drawing the map of India at the assembly of Shaheen Bagh? It was a time of deeply chilling and deeply reassuring experiences. The protests left their imprint on the mind that cannot be wiped out easily. We may need carbon dating to read those prints on the bones in the future.

What Does a Protest Look Like?

Under the garb of national security, the state enforces a zone of silence that aims at silencing all kinds of protests. Dalit protests or farmer protests, hence, should not be seen in isolation. The Dalit protests were not just about the annulation of the SC-ST Acts or against Rohith Vemula's death, but it was also about the immoral institutions and the failure of the justice mechanisms. The farmers' protest was not just about the farms and fields but also about restoring the fundamental right to protest. These protests, in a broader context, enrich democratic values. They complement and strengthen each other. Berger would say that a protest is not only about a sacrifice for a just future. It is also about 'an inconsequential redemption of the present'.[8] These protests renewed the act of

---

[7] Zeynep Tufecki, 'Do Protests Even Work', *The Atlantic*, 24 June 2020. https://www.theatlantic.com/technology/archive/2020/06/why-protests-work/613420/

[8] Berger, *Bento's Sketchbook*, 113.

redemption and the zeal for life and resistance. Let us celebrate the small victory against a culture of silence and breathlessness prevailing around us.

Some of these protests came after death, destruction, and a lingering wait. They bloomed after a gloom like a smile after tears; through a tearful smile, they came. Cry if you feel, but smile because it is so beautiful. They created sights to behold. The farmers' protest in Delhi was one such protest. Daring, beautiful, organized, and unshakable. Its zeal was difficult to capture. Language fails us. I am just trying to capture the spirit that I have seen. It was something extraordinary. I saw the march of the mustard in one of the largest farmer protests in Indian history.

March of the Mustard

Mustard was blooming on the barricades; marigolds were dancing on the borders. The kernels of maize had found carnal desire in the alliance of bodies. Full of red and green, yellow and cream, in orange and black, they were back. The protest brought back a full-blown smile on the faces that the state had stolen from us.

They marched. From Amritsar, Jalandhar, Patiala, Moga, Taran Taran.[9] They came marching like the march of the forest in *Macbeth*. As Birnam Wood had marched to Dunsinane Hill, the paddy field marched to Raisina Hill. It was an exchange of roses and marigolds on the borders. Red met orange, and green met blue. Paddy fields danced with water cannons and bodies with batons. They came marching with banners and flags, with legs and lags, in *pagadi* (turban), in salwar, in pyjama, and *turra* (headdress). They came marching on the rhythm of the *giddha* and the *bhangra* (local dance forms); on the rhythm of the *nagara* (drum).

They faced the barricades. They faced the blockades. They faced the batons. They were sanitized with tear gas and sewage

---

[9] All these Punjab districts saw a huge participation of people in the farmers' protest in Delhi.

water. But they were determined to reach Delhi. A farmer said, 'we will die but we will go to Delhi'. The state tried all tricks to stop them. It tried to crush them. It tried to cut the blossoming flowers as it did with the Muslim protestors in Shaheen Bagh. But do the state and authorities have the knife to cut the poetry of life? Perhaps not. If they come to cut the flowers again, one can evoke Pablo Neruda, 'You can cut all the flowers, but you can't stop spring from coming'. Whatever they do, *vasant* (spring) will come. They came prepared to celebrate Baisakhi and Lohri (popular harvest festivals from Punjab) in Delhi.

Covered in green and yellow, they marched as fields were marching. They marched as crop were marching; they marched as wheat was marching. They marched as soil and sweat were marching. Pulsating in their bodies, pulses came marching. Gram secured its nose and marched. With a torn belly, wheat joked to bajra: what else can they do to me? In the wee hours, they marched like butterflies. At night, they marched like fireflies. At noon, they marched with the sun. In the evening, they marched with the moon. They marched singing the song of Sant Ram Udasi: '*Maa dharteye, teri godh nu chann hor bathere*' (O mother earth, in your lap, there are a million moons).[10] They marched this time to cut their harvest in Delhi.

Perhaps they had come decided: if they could not breathe in the field, they would burn *parali* (stubble) in Delhi to choke the breath of the city. When the fields burn, then the city will not be a safe haven. You will be choked by the smoke that engulfs the fields. You cannot talk about climate change when the fields and forests are burning, when there is farmer unrest, and farms are under arrest by corporates.

They marched. They marched with trucks and trollies. When

---

[10] Sant Ram Udasi (1939–1986) was a major Punjabi poet who came from a Dalit background and shaped a new sensibility of Punjabi poetry through his use of vernacular language mixed with deep sensitivity and radical politics.

they spread their tents, it appeared as though villages were marching. The fields came marching with flowers and leaves, trees and branches, and with the thorns of roses. In the age of visuals that blind and bind us together, the march showed us that the soil still is the source of colour. The colours still have names and figures, such as mango and brinjal, such as maize and *mahua* (oil nut).

A nation obsessed with the Wagah-Attari border with Pakistan came to know about the Singhu, Tikri, and Ghazipur borders of Delhi. The borders that exist but are not recognized; the borders that separate the classes but are not seen. The caste borders that remain at large. The borders that divide the village and the city; the invisible borders of the CCTV cameras and security infrastructure. The border surrounding the parliament where people are not allowed to enter. The protest made them all visible. Cracks opened up. What also became visible is that national boundaries are not the map of the nation. Borders are in the form of cracks, rifts, and leaks in the field — in the cracked heels of the farmers. The heel holds many maps together, more complex than the map of a nation.

A protest can be issue-based, but it is never about itself alone. Neither was Shaheen Bagh just about the citizenship bill nor was the farmers' protest just about the farms. Protest is the name of plurality. It is the name of multitudes. It comes from many directions. It goes in many directions. It unfolds in the unknown. It is always about many things: it is about the farms, but it is also about women leading from the front. It is about the alliances between bread and the moon, necessity and desire.

March like Margins

Despite their differences, the farmers' protest, the Shaheen Bagh protest, and the Dalit protests were very special. They brought together the assembly of people who are usually considered apolitical and on the margin. The bodies belonging to the private sphere — women, children, and the old — came out into the public square. What was considered 'gossip' was indeed political. The march of the *nanis* and *dadis* (grandmothers) and the walk of the grandchildren were not part of some reality show. Young Dalit protestors throwing carcasses in front of government offices and refusing to carry away dead cows during the Una protests in Gujarat indicated a new signal. It was the demonstration of new bodies and subjects. It was the birth of new politics. It was an event of walking and protesting that will rewrite history in the coming days.

A protest does not end in immediacy. It travels unknown paths. It leaves footprints. It leaves its shadow. People remember the Mahad Satyagrah led by Ambedkar, and they remember the farmers' protest led by Mahendra Singh Tikait. The Chengara struggle entered history. Shaheen Bagh is not yet dead. They are the name of the spirits. The spirits appeared on the Tikri border. Mahindar Kaur of the farmers' protest indeed carries the spirit of Bilkis Bano of the anti-CAA-NRC protest. They carry the spirit of each other. They greet each other. They meet each other whenever they march. It is the march of the minorities that connects them.

A protest is the name of the folding, unfolding, and holding of bodies together. It is the name of the assembly that exists outside the parliament. It is what Berger says is saving 'the present moment, whatever the future holds'.[11] It is also about reclaiming the past, not the glory of war and conquests, but of the dissents and discontents.

A protest is the name of critical encounters — an encounter that can lead to injury or that can lead to birth, life, and death. An encounter can be termed fake — such as a fake police encounter. A protest is the name of the possibilities that hold our fate. A protest is a site where politics enunciates; it creates a dialogue in which

[11] John Berger, *Bento's Sketchbook*, 95.

principles are agreed upon, solidarity is formed, and alliances are forged. It is about the sit-in of the bodies and the setting of the ideas in an out-and-out experiment. You fall, you fail, but you rise and protest. It is about the bodies on the barricades.

A protest posits the precarious condition of life. We can understand in what condition one might have to come out to participate in protests during the time of the pandemic: when you have an emergency, when you cannot breathe, when you do not have time to hear an actor's dramatized speech, when you do not have time to dial the designated number, when you know that they do not have a treatment for your illness. If some things are equally precious to life, they are love and protest. Both are banned and, therefore, protest is special. The coronavirus can be life-threatening, but one can risk life for freedom and rights.

A protest spills out ink on the smooth black-and-white surfaces of history. History is not black and white. It is not a sheet of paper lying in the archives. History is a grain of wheat. It has the colour of mustard, green and yellow, but it can turn red and black when it seeds. 'I protest' is not a simple utterance. It is the name of politics. It is a deep cut into history. It is a cease, it is a break, it is newness, and it cannot become normative. A protest is the poetry of life. It is an unparalleled utterance. 'I protest' is the only authentic relation of politics — a pure and uncontaminated one.

Any movement will have its weaknesses and shortcomings. Let's celebrate the spirit of the march that laid siege to Delhi. It was the citizens denied who laid the siege. It was an indefinite blockade that compelled the authorities to come to the table. It was the seige that the state saw as anti-national.

Protest is the reinvention and re-creation of life. It is not a market slogan for performance or else that will recreate life. It is a case of protest or perish. It is the insistence of politics. It is the persistence of life. It is the resistance of the body. It is the coming of the assembly. It is the formation of alliances that define rights and democracy. Protest against the figure of authority, protest against imposition, protest against the curfew. Protest for life and the freedom of the mind.

And it says that they protested!

'The Revolution Will Not Be Televised'

They protested. They were emboldened. They thought that they would emerge as heroes. They thought that the media would televise their revolution. They remembered the slogan but forgot the song that the revolution will not be televised.

You will not be able to stay home, brother
You will not be able to plug in, turn on and cop out [...]
And skip out for beer[*tea*] during commercials, because
The revolution will not be televised.

There will be no highlights on the eleven [*nine*] o'clock news
And no pictures of hairy armed women liberationists
[...] The revolution will not be televised.[12]

Gil Scott-Heron's words ring true even today. We can tune into them for some time as a break from Twitter and our TV sets. This is a song for all those who thought that the biggest protest of our time — the farmers' protest — would be televised on prime time. The song is a reminder of the reality of the protest and resistance and the limits of what can be televised and what cannot. The song is too raw, but it is too real. Take it literally; nothing will be televised. Neither your rage, nor your death, nor your life, nor your breathlessness.

The assertion that the revolution or protest will not be televised is both political and ontological in a sense. They are the name of the radical ruptures that make the world upside-down. They are the moments of an outbreak that cannot be framed. They are not

[12] Gil Scott-Heron, 'The Revolution Will Not Be Televised', https://www. historyisaweapon.com/defcon1/herontelevised.html

channels that can be channelized. Protestors have to risk their body and space, violently or non-violently. One can capture the gesture, one can capture the posture, but the protest remains at large to linger in future movements and memories.

During the farmers' protest in Delhi, when the farmers' union leaders and the authorities negotiated the route, they must have thought that the people would obey the command and follow the designated route. However, they forget that a protest cannot be routed. They forget that people are not armies or dancers whose movements are choreographed.

You were wrong if you thought that the revolution would be televised at prime time at 9 p.m. If you had thought that your handshake, your smile, your shout, your laughing out loud would be televised, you were wrong. That your love, your *langar* (free-of-charge community kitchens), your warmth, your ways of winning the hearts of Delhi would be televised, you were wrong. It was wrong on your part to believe that your protest on the ground would shake the nation's conscience. You were wrong if you thought that mass action spoke louder than the rowdy media. You won on the ground but lacked the narrative. You had the moment but failed in the media. And a successful protest failed in the narrative.

Media and the Mobs

What happened on 26 January 2021 was astounding. The day began with parallel parades. When elected representatives were busy ritualizing the republic, it felt as if the republic had slipped into the streets to greet the people. As the nation showcased its success and might, the farmers came to show their plight. As the imported jet roared in the air to show the power of the self-reliant nation, one who made the nation self-reliant (on food) was standing on the road.

The battle began. One had the power, the other had the people. One had the nation, the other had the land. One had the media, the other had the message. The one who was voted for held the centre, the one who voted had to go to the borders (peripheries). It went deeper. Separated, barricaded, full of trenches, diving deep into the skin and psyche: the nation and the farmer! One who grows, one who rips; one who sweats, one who sleeps; one who sells, one who sacrifices. The cut was so deep that the boundaries within the borders appeared natural.

On 26 January 2021, I joined the farmers' protest near the Tikri border, where one of the major groups was holding a sit-in. My Republic Day zeal was back after a long time. I remember we enthusiastically participated in the event during our school days. We passed from one border to another, encircling Delhi. Delhi borders were all mesmerizing. It was offering oblation to the farmers with slogans and flowers, spreading the message of love, discarding hate. It appeared as if the farmers had returned after winning a world cup. There were celebrations all around: marching tractors, biking protestors, slogan-shouting women reminding one of the liberationists of the 60s, cheering crowds, dancing children, the love and warmth of the locals spreading the contagious courage amidst the warning of the spread of the coronavirus. Protestors might not have expected the response they received. It was overwhelming.

The newness of the protest overshadowed the ritual parade of the neoliberal state. The message was clear: it was neither only the parade nor only the parallel show. It was a battle between the fake and the real, between the obsession for power and the passionate articulation of the people. Said an onlooker, the protest would bring the government down. However, things unfolded another way.

While these were the scenes on the streets, something else was unfolding on the screens. The mainstream media was going berserk. While the protest remained largely peaceful on the ground, the media created monsters all around. The media plotted the narrative as a dictator plots a dictatorship. Far from the real and in the time of post-truth, visuals created visibility and repetitions created referentiality. The media successfully proved that the protest was a threat to sovereignty.

The media presented farmers as mobs — unruly and uncivilized, a barbaric community taking down civility. As targets were turned into threats, the elite and middle classes' repulsion for the farmers was evident. Against the tractors and trolleys, trolls came out. Creepy anchors crept into hatred and leaders into hate speech. In a largely agricultural nation, farmers were called unruly, anti-social, goons, hoodlums, and anti-nationals. When their family members in the army were getting medals for bravery from the government, they received badges of shame. The caste mind came out. The farmers' touch desecrated the monument's sacredness in the nation's Brahminical body politic. In demonizing and witch-hunting the farmers, the nation re-actualized the centre. The plot brought down the biggest protest of our times.

Those who thought that the liberal media would cover the protest were stunned after seeing their balancing act on the rope. The media deployed their language in the most innocent way. Goondas were called locals, and farmers were called foreigners. When the police and goondas attacked a peaceful gathering, they named it a clash. The group that talked about freedom was termed a mob. When the state kills people, it is a 'riot'. When people defend themselves, it is called 'obstruction of duty'. The use of such language by the media becomes proof for the police. This shows how much the media can manipulate, how much they can manufacture, how cold-bloodedly they can crush, and how fatal they can be.

It matters how we describe and define protests. It matters how a protest is projected. The curtailment of protests also happens in the writings and reporting on protests. Descriptions such as the 'police clashed with students', 'mayhem', and 'chaos' try to delegitimize the moral standing of the protestors. In 'Don't Fall for the "Chaos" Theory of the Protests', Megan Garber writes that 'language matters and framings matter'.[13] Let us develop a framework to see how we want to see protests.

Though it is difficult to say who is more policed, the police or the media, because while the police fired tear gas, the media fired the culture bomb. Without firing a bullet, they annihilated the confidence of the protestors in themselves. Their every 'shot' shot down the power of non-violence. Every shot was a manipulation of the truth. Every shot propelled a lie. Every shot was the ammunition of hate. Every shot was a shot in the arm of the authoritarian state. Every shot was fired to sustain the narrative of the state. Every shot was a shot of betrayal and something that will lie in the hearts of protestors for years. History should remember how a historical protest was made to fail by the media and popular narrative.

The farmers' unions were wrong if they thought the media would give them a standing ovation for taking moral responsibility for the violence. They were wrong if they thought the protest could be routed like a parade. They assumed people would move on the assigned path without deviating from its route. It was certainly named a parade, but it was an out-and-out protest. It did what every protest does — disruption. Instead of asking for sympathy, it marked a non-violent assertion.

The protest shook not only the state but also the conscience of the union leaders who wanted to organize the protest to mobilize sympathy and not claims — the claim that the city also belongs to us. It would be disastrous to think that a non-violent protest is an act of pleading and not a matter of assertion. The state has termed all such assertions an act of violence. One is not advocating for a violent protest; one is merely asking to go beyond the state's definition of violence and non-violence and read the Republic Day parade in that light.

[13] Megan Garber, 'Don't Fall for the "Chaos" Theory of the Protests', *The Atlantic*, https://www.theatlantic.com/culture/archive/2020/06/george-floyd-protests-are-not-chaos-trump-new-york-times/612544/ /

Peaceful Protest and Anti-Social Violence

What we witnessed on 26 January 2021 was a farmers' upsurge in Delhi. In a situation of upsurge, it is too much to ask people to follow the route. The farmer leaders succumbed to the hegemonic media narrative; it appeared that they were not prepared for the psychological war waged by the media and the state. Imagine what could have happened if the union leaders had taken bold positions, claiming the protest's success, justifying the protestors' actions, and blaming the government for the violence. It might have looked unethical to many, but the movement could have been more intact. The activists would have been more emboldened. It could have been difficult for the state to go for the assault they initiated in the aftermath of 26 January. So, shall one give up moral conscience and just think from the standpoint of morality when life itself is at risk?

The other points that can be raised are: when was the last time the Delhi Police apologized for their violent acts? When was the last time the Home Minister apologized for the riots? Anyone who has participated in peaceful protests in Delhi knows how the police provoke violence, how they throw stones at peaceful protestors, how they use water cannons with sewage water, how they arrange local goondas in masks and helmets to beat the protestors, how they kick women protestors in the belly. They do not apologize because the state thinks that it has a monopoly on violence. It can do what it wants. The liability of non-violence always lies with the other.

The point is not so much about how the state manipulates violence and non-violence to enhance its power. The more serious problem is that the state has a monopoly on violence, and the police force has been propped up in popular perception. So, while a peaceful protest and demonstration is called violent, state violence is seen as an act of maintaining peace, such as a surveillance camera for security. After the 26 January event, the

Delhi Police placed concrete walls and iron nails on the roads so that the protestors could not move. In an interview, the police said that they carved the iron nails on the road to maintain peace and facilitate the way for peaceful protestors.[14]

The question is not merely about the practice of violence but how violence and non-violence are defined and who defines them. Judith Butler argues that the state seeks to rename non-violent practices as violent.[15] It is done at the level of public semantics. Often, the one who claims to practice non-violence also misses these nuances and gets easily entrapped in the statist understanding of violence. This brings us to the point at which every peaceful protest has been named violent in recent years in India. Many times, the police and the state-sponsored goons deliberately tried to provoke the protestors to show that they, protestors, were violent.

One should also ask a basic question: When was the last time a peaceful protest did not turn 'violent'? Was Shaheen Bagh not labelled as a terrorists' assembly? These instances clearly show that violence and non-violence do not depend on acts but on the authority that names them. So, should one not condemn violence in peaceful protests? One should. But condemning violence of any sort is a trap. The increasingly passive sense of non-violence needs a more nuanced approach before we declare peacefully protesting farmers as anti-social elements.

The question of non-violence has to be re-articulated not from the position of a privileged sense of morality, but from the extreme sense of vulnerability, from the exposed point of the iron nails, from the point of 'I can't breathe' and 'I can't move'. The question of non-violence has to be reposited when the authority does not have a conscience, when it keeps posing the logic of non-violence for others and none for itself. Otherwise, there is a danger that we

[14] https://www.thehindu.com/news/national/farmers-protest-iron-nails-fixed-on-roads-at-ghazipur-border-being-repositioned-delhi-police/article33748321.ece

[15] Judith Butler, *Precarious Life: The Powers of Mourning and Violence.* Verso, 2004.

accept the very idea of the protest and demonstration as a violent act — the stated statist position.

One needs to read the message and intention inherent in the so-called violent and non-violent act. In Martin Luther King Jr's words, 'A riot is the language of unheard'.[16] Though one cannot romanticize this idea of the riot, one needs to read the message from the point of vulnerability and desperation. The use of water cannons, the firing of tear gas, barricading assigned routes, the police lathi-charging — have all been accepted to facilitate peaceful protestors. It has been accepted that placing the barricade is a part of maintaining peace, but removing or pushing it amounts to an act of violence.

There is no doubt that sporadic violence happened during the farmers' protest. But the protest's more sustained and powerful criticisms came for another reason: the symbolic violence through which a group of farmers entered the Red Fort. Can we term their act as an act of anti-social elements? The media and the middle-class understanding of violence and non-violence are like vegetarianism and non-vegetarianism. The one who eats vegetables is non-violent, while the one who is non-vegetarian is violent. Neither the question of violence nor the practice of non-violence can be simplified to this level.

A Matter of Visibility than Violence

Is there any other way in which one can read the farmers entering the Red Fort? One can read the act of farmers entering the Red Fort more as a matter of visibility than violence; it was more a matter of owning than disowning. It was more a matter of right than the rite through which one reads it as an act of discretion. Maybe one group worked as instigators. However, for several of

---

[16] Peter Weber, '"A Riot is the Language of the Unheard": Martin Luther King Jr explained 53 years ago', *The Week*, 29 May 2020. https://theweek.com/speedreads/917022/riot-language-unheard-martin-luther-king-jr-explained-53-years-ago

the protestors, entering the monument was a sacred act and a symbol of pride. It cannot be read as storming or capturing the Red Fort. By participating in the act, some farmers made a simple point that the national symbol belongs to all. If the farmers' touch of the Red Fort is read as an act of sacrilege, then the interpretation has only one logic. It comes from untouchability. It is nothing but a casteist interpretation.

For the farmers who entered the Red Fort, it was more a matter of appearance than occupation. It was more a matter of citizenship than terrorism. It was more an act of democracy than a disturbance. It was more a matter of forceful non-violence than violence. It was a matter of reclaiming the space that we had already lost. We have already lost the very sense of non-violence. After 60 days of protest, it was a desperate attempt to demonstrate one's grievances when the state lost its conscience. The protest failed not because they turned 'violent' but because even the practice of non-violence was perceived and termed as violent. Even sporadic violence becomes a seditious act with a chargeable offence. When a joke itself is perceived as a threat, we need to redefine non-violence.

7. A Siege Against the Siege

The Larger Significance of the Una Strike

The Strike

We want to feel the sunshine
And we want to smell the flow'rs
We are sure that God has willed it
And we mean to have eight hours;
We're summoning our forces
From the shipyard, shop and mill

Eight hours for work,
Eight hours for rest
Eight hours for what we will.[1]

'Eight Hours' is a beautiful memory of the glorious history of the workers' strike. It was not technology, horology, astrology, or the movement of the sun or stars, but it was the workers' strike that changed the sense of time in modern history. It was the slaves' strike that sent the sun to set. Otherwise, the sun set neither for the empire nor the slaves. Shudras and slave never had their own time. Work time, rest time, holidays, and weekends look so natural today, but they weren't always a right. Workers brought down the hours by the brute force of a strike. They did it by putting their bodies on the barricades: participating in a siege, refusing to work and creating a situation of a 'riot'.

---

[1] The song 'Eight Hours' was written by I.G. Blanchard and composed by Rev. Jesse Jones, originally published in 1878. It became the rallying song of the eight hours working day movement.

On 1 May 1886, hundreds of thousands of workers laid siege to the railroads and factories in the United States. They halted the machines. They shut down the factory gates. They blocked the movement. They seized time and history. They gave a slogan that resonated like a song. 'Eight hours for work / Eight hours for rest / Eight hours for what we will.' The legacy of the May Day strike is beautiful as well as explosive. It is explosively beautiful. Its beauty lies in its radicalism. But how do we think of a strike at a time when the authoritarian regime is criminalizing peaceful protests? They labelled the peaceful anti-CAA protest as an 'anti-national' assembly. They called the farmers' movement a 'terrorist' gathering. The Una strike in Gujarat in 2016 brought back the question of strikes again. When rights and dissents were facing curtailment, it renewed its commitment to the strike. Strike that can be termed as bare minimum protest.

In the Una strike, India witnessed one of the most powerful and aesthetic modes of protest in recent history. It remains unparalleled in its evocation and precariousness. It used actions that were unsettling to the authorities. It deployed the art of disgust that was repulsive to the Hindu social order. The artwork of Una stood against the notion of purity. It unleashed danger at a sublime level. It appeared with terror and awe. It exposed the hypocrisy of Hinduism. But its larger significance seemed to be much larger than what it did. It has to do with how you strike to make a strike meaningful in a specific cultural context.

If the larger significance of the Bhima Koregaon lies in the fact that the Dalits can defeat the upper-caste Peshwas by challenging caste supremacy, the larger significance of the Una strike lies in the fact that a caste society can be seized and Hindu society can be put on hold. It also indicates that the mode of strike that works in one part of the world may not work in other parts. While taking the knee as a symbolic mode of protest has been quite successful in the USA, it has symbolically failed in India. It also says that the mode of protest that works for one gender and class may not work for others. Some modes are more accessible to women and the lower castes. Some modes of protest only privilege civil society. The Una strike placed the question of cultural significance at the centre. It was one of the most ingenious, indigenous, and integral strikes in India's recent history.

Let's start with fundamentals. Was the Una protest a 'general strike' or a 'general protest'? Does it matter? It matters. It matters for various reasons. It matters, foremost, for the mode of the strike itself. A strike as a mode of protest has been facing massive curtailment from the neoliberal authoritarian regime. It is becoming less common as the new laws and work contracts make it impossible. *The irony.* We are living in a time of ceaseless work. We are living in the age of the impossibility of the strike. To embark on the Una strike is also to expand the notion of the strike itself. It is about the tension and contention that makes the right to protest a fundamental right in India. The right to strike is a legal right with limitations. Indian laws only give this right to registered trade unions. So, register before you go on strike. Form a union before you go on strike. But if you are thinking of forming a union or unionizing the workers, the authorities will be hell-bent on crushing you as if you have been founding a terrorist organization. Basically, you can't form a union. You can't go on strike. Thus, whether the Una strike was a strike poses a real question.

The notion of a strike, though changed, remains confined to the workers' questions. But, how do we place women's, contractual labourers', and sanitation workers' strikes? How do we place daily wage labourers and migrant workers? How do we place the workers who are not on professional contracts? Neither are workers called workers, nor are owners called owners. They appear as *kameen* (service providers) and *jajman*s (patrons) in a caste society, and zamindars (feudal lords) and *raiyat*s (servitudes) in a feudal society. They may appear as wives and husbands in a household. They can be singers, dancers, or entertainers who beg but don't receive wages. They appear as sweepers and cleaners but not as workers and staff. As they say in Delhi, we have five staff and one sweeper.

On the other side, it was the women's strike for equality that gave them the equal right to vote. The great anti-slavery scholar and activist W.E.B. Du Bois famously described the American Civil War as a 'General Strike'.[2] In India, Ambedkar wanted to see the Mahars (Dalits) organize a 'general strike' against the Watan system in Maharashtra.[3] Rosa Luxemburg placed much emphasis on the theory of the general strike rather than the strike organized by political workers. All this may look like a forced connection, but they are so telling on strikes.

Perhaps they all saw the 'general strike' as what Rosa Luxemburg termed 'a means of inaugurating the social revolution'. She viewed the general strike 'in contradistinction to the daily political struggle of the working-class'.[4] Despite their varied concerns, they all were committed to the social revolution. What does it mean? It means besides organized workers, other sections have also used strikes as a method.

When we had almost given up the strike as a method, the Una strike came with full force. It asked us, how is it that we cannot strike? How is it that we are giving up this mode of protest and making the working class more vulnerable? While civil society will continue to protest with some curtailments, what will workers do, if not strike? Should they be shut up in their workplaces?

More than a protest, a strike is a mode of communication in an unequal exchange. Precisely for this reason, strikes remain vital — a reassuring and fire-giving force for the oppressed. Strikes bring not only better wages and work conditions but also dignity and freedom. It makes dialogue democratic beyond the *jee huzuri* (Yes, boss) culture. A strike is important. It is important to strike. Strike

---

² W.E.B. Du Bois, *Black Reconstruction in America, 1860-1880* (New York: Routledge, 2012) [1935], 49-73.

³ B.R. Ambedkar, *BAWS*, Vol. 2, 87.

⁴ Rosa Luxemburg, *The Mass Strike, marxist.org*, https://www.marxists.org/archive/luxemburg/1906/mass-strike/ch01.htm

differently, different strikes. People do strike for different reasons. Strike!

Before any communist movement came onto the scene, Jyotiba Phule and Savitri Phule led the barbers' strike against the custom of shaving the heads of Brahmin widows in Maharashtra in 1827. On 6 April 1919, Gandhi called for a *hartal* (strike) against the Rowlatt Act. It was an act to detain and imprison someone without trial indefinitely — a UAPA of its time. Histories of communist movements are full of strikes, from workers' strikes to farmers' strikes, from union strikes to strikes to form a union and beyond. Ambedkar's Labour Party organized many labour strikes. His party formed alliances with the communist unions to organize strikes. But they also had fallouts. I'm not interested in their relationship here. What I am interested in is the principle, power, and necessity of the strike itself. I am interested in how the authoritarian regime is trying to demonize it. I recall Ambedkar, who defended the strike on principles. On the same principles, he fought the cases for the strikers who were part of the communist unions despite his differences.

Strike: A Breach of Contract

Ambedkar engages with the question of the strike in such a threadbare way. From the basic question of what a strike is, how it relates to the right to freedom, to how it is not an act of conspiracy, he discusses its various facets. What is a strike? He says that a 'strike is nothing more than a breach of contract of service'.[5] He underlines that 'when a worker strikes, all that it means is that he commits a breach of contract of service: there is nothing more in it, and nothing less in it'.[6] A breach of contract of service is not a crime by Indian laws. He argues that 'to make it a crime would

---

[5] B.R. Ambedkar, *BAWS*, Vol. 2, 87.
[6] Ibid.

be to compel a man to serve against his will'.[7] He contends that to penalize a strike, therefore, is nothing short of making a worker a slave. He views the right to strike as inseparable from the right to freedom.

> It has been said that there is no such thing as the right to strike. My reply is that this statement can come from a man who really does not understand what a strike is. If members are prepared to accept my meaning of the word 'strike' as being nothing more than a breach of contract, then I submit that a strike is simply another name for the right to freedom; it is nothing else than the right to the freedom of one's services on any terms that one wants to obtain.[8]

He goes on to say that if we once concede the right to freedom, we also concede the right to strike. In a leap of speech, he asserts, 'If you accept that the right to freedom is a divine right, then I contend that the right to strike is a divine right'.[9] He fires a salvo against the house members who were planning to curtail the strike. He says that snatching the right to strike would mean the workers would not have civil rights. In such a situation, don't call it the 'Industrial Disputes Bill'; better name it the 'Workers' Civil Liberties Suspension Act'. The curtailment of this right, in his words, will 'bring perpetual slavery to workers'. He goes on in his evocative speech. He ends his remarks with another blast, 'If this is not a Bill for introducing slavery amongst workers, I would like to know what sort of Bill would introduce slavery'.[10]

Ambedkar's exposition has become more relevant today as we see increasing restrictions and near banning of strikes. What is important in Ambedkar's formulation is strike as 'the breach

---

[7] B.R. Ambedkar, *BAWS*, Vol. 2, 207.

[8] B.R. Ambedkar, *BAWS*, Vol. 2, 208.

[9] B.R. Ambedkar, *BAWS*, Vol. 2, 208.

[10] B.R. Ambedkar, *BAWS*, Vol. 2, 211.

of contract of service'. 'Nothing' is vital here. 'Nothing more' and 'nothing less' than a breach of contract of service. This is an interesting negative formulation. 'Nothing' is not really about 'nothing'. It is about opening up enormous possibilities. What happens in a breach of any contract? A party refuses to follow the rules. If a party refuses to follow the rules, the game is over. In a more extreme case, it may lead to the collapse of a system. What will happen in caste society when Dalits or lower castes or, for that matter, women breach this social contract? It will be a transgression. Crossing the *lakshman rekha*. The Una strike was an act of nothing but breaching the social contract. They breached it by refusing to follow the caste rules. The slogan, 'Cow is your mother, you perform the last rite', was a performative utterance for that breach of contract.

The unwritten social contract usually doesn't allow the so-called lower caste to violate these rules. One of the meanings of Shudra is that they should serve without resentment. Ambedkar's strike — *not more than a breach of contract* — opens up a whole canvas of possibilities. Only when one breaches the contract does one know one's capacity: what else can one do? Breaches often open up new vistas of freedom. Freedom in art is fundamentally about the breaches.

A strike — a direct militant action — remains the most powerful defence in the hands of the working class across the world. This is also a reason that it is facing a backlash, both at the ideological level as well in physical actions. There has been an attempt to discredit and criminalize this powerful mode of protest. It is not surprising that a strike often gets equated with a riot. It is not only criminalized by the authorities but also in the larger domain of democratic culture. The corporate regime calls it violent. Analysts call it violent. Civil society tends to denounce it. The term, strike, is becoming a parlance of military language. In recent years, the Indian authorities have talked more about the Balakot strike than the workers' strike, and the militants' strike in

Pulwama than the Maruti workers' strike in Manesar.[11] From the point of meeting our demand or we will go on strike to the point of 'perform or else', workers' movements are on the backfoot.

A strike is another name for refusal. A strike usually happens in a formal relationship. How do we read the Una strike where there is no formal contract? But the contract is already ritualized. That makes it more formal. The refusal becomes more difficult. One is not only refusing a secular authority but is also against religions and customs. You are refusing the demigods that may follow you in your dreams. A strike is a refusal with an affirmation in which one appears in politics. The refusal is political.

Refusal is a break. It is about breathing space. It is about the pause in which you tilt the position of the Big Others. Its beauty lies not in performance but in the assertion that we will not perform any longer. *We will not work. We will not move.* In a strike, a pause is a declaration of freedom. The public declaration in Una that we will not perform or we will not observe the rites marked this refusal. The refusal created a crisis in existing social relationships. If it didn't break them, it created a crack in the ritualized bond that was there for a long time.

Such refusal often faces the burnt of the caste society. Upon Ambedkar's call, Dalits refused to eat meat from carcasses in Maharashtra in 1927. It led to the protest by the dominant Maratha communities. They threatened them that 'they will be driven out of the villages if they do not eat carcasses'. They asked them 'not to transgress their customary social limits'.[12] Exactly the same happened in parts of Gujarat when Dalit communities decided that they would not skin the dead cow. *The irony.* Upper castes flogged them when they were skinning the dead cows. Now they

---

[11] The Maruti Suzuki plant at Manesar in Haryana has been in the news for workers' strikes for years now.

[12] Krupa Desai, 'Mahad Satyagraha (1927) and Gandhi's 21 Day Fast in Poona (1933): Political Acts-Events-Performance' (MPhil Thesis, Jawaharlal Nehru University, New Delhi, 2015), 148.

were threatening them because they refused to skin and depose the carcasses.

A strike is a protest that is not marked by movements but by pauses and breaks. It is about creating breathing space. It is about creating a new awareness of the body and relationships. It is about time to pause and reflect. After the pause, you stop seeing the ways you used to see. Things do not appear in the same way. Eyes get a new lens. The one who participates finds a new perspective.

A strike is a cessation against a constant performance, endless repetition of a machine, the infectious imitation of the caste system. If a protest is about moving bodies and rising hands, the strike is about a pause that appears as a gesture. It is about the pause that marks our postures. You pause, and a gesture emerges. When bodies pause, posture emerges. The strike is about positionality. It is the pause that creates events in history. The pause can be momentary, it can become breath-taking; it can become a memento of life.

A strike forefronts the fundamental expression of life and work. It becomes the last resort of the workers and the people on the margins. By demonizing the strike, the market regime has made the workers defenceless. But a loss of strike is not only the question of the loss of a mode of protest. It can be seen as the loss of the last expression of the oppressed.

In pragmatic terms, the loss is not possible because the people who will get exploited will also strike. But the danger is that we may lose its space in democratic expression. Civil society will protest peacefully. But what will workers do? Do we think that owners will hear their pleas? Do we think that they can sign and circulate the petition and negotiate with power? Do we think that they will speak out about their oppression in this precarious condition?

Without the right to strike, the power has shut up the workers in their workplaces. We rarely see workers coming out to protest. We barely see workers in public spaces. We hardly hear workers speaking of their harsh conditions, even if they are harassed every hour. We think that all's well with the workers. They wear the company logo and make their 'choices' in the free market. Even if they are dying of suffocation, we think that they are in heaven. A strike exposes this real condition.

A strike is the name of concerted action resulting in the cessation of work. Wheels will not move unless our demand comes. Unlike demonstrations that largely carry a symbolic value, a strike is also a real physical act. Neither is the body the only metaphor here nor the barricades. It is the name of an open confrontation both at the physical and symbolic levels. Its effect is immediate. It is an act of showdown and slowdown together. A strike is an organized cease against an organized sin. Other protests are about marches and sit-ins, but a strike is about laying siege. A performance against performance. An anti-performance act.

The strike underlines a high moral and ethical ground. It comes in the workers' claim. *You may own the factory, but we will not allow you to enter the factory gate.* It carries the ethical sense of ownership of production. It is the 'we' who run it with our sweat and blood. It is 'we' — the cheap labourers working in dangerous conditions — who are your surplus. It is the 'we' who produce; it is the 'we' who are threatened. In a strike, one risks the space because one cares. One strikes because one is in a desperate situation.

The strike has been the radical legacy of the workers, but it is not limited to them. A strike can happen wherever there is an exploitation of relationships. Within the household, women and children go on strike for smaller demands in traditional societies. Children go on strike for toys. A wife may say, 'Don't touch me if you cannot bring me a new saree'. It happens. Love and sex strikes are not uncommon. Those spaces are not just about playful games of the two sexes; they are also about rights, dignity, and respect. I have seen a woman saying that '*main tumhara baccha paida karne wali machine nahin hun*' (I am not your birth-giving machine). I want to stop.

Strike in Caste Society

Strike as a term is common to the workers but is rarely discussed in relation to caste, despite the fact that caste and labour are so connected and the connection is striking. You tell me your caste, and I can tell you what kinds of work you do. Caste works as occupation with religious sanctions. Thus, strike in caste society is also a critique of religion. Unlike other creation myths of human societies, the Hindu creation myth is less about the birth of the 'man' (human being) and more about the division of the man at birth.

The *Purusha Sukta* tells us a story in which Purusha (cosmic man) is sacrificed for the sake of division. The man was killed in the primordial sacrifice so the society of high caste and varna could be formed. When the primordial man died, the caste demons appeared from different parts of his body. The Brahmins emerged from the mouth, the Kshatriya from the arms, Vaishya from the thighs, and Shudra from the feet. We know the story. The division of work is based on the division of the body. It is not your birth, but your rebirth that gives you a higher status. Some are once-born, and some are twice-born. Some take birth time and again and become avatars to defend this division. Therefore, it is important to strike both in material contexts, but also in the domain of religion.

Caste society maintains a persistent siege on the body and space. Where can one move, where one cannot, what one can perform, what one cannot? Your rights, your duties, and the success of your life and death are already destined unless you deviate. Caste keeps performing this structure, confirming it, reaffirming it through different mechanisms, from rituals to sanctions, from lynching to violence, through repetitions, imitations, and performances. It creates a reciprocal system in which both the upper castes and the lower castes participate. They create an unwritten contract of services. The day the other side does not participate, caste will cease to exist. It will cease to perform. It will be dead within days. But this precisely does not happen. The existing social structure does not allow it to happen. But many times, this possibility spills over. It happened during the Una strike.

If Hindu society behaves like a gang that takes society for ransom, Dalits during the Una strike took them on hold. Within a few days, it brought Hindu society to its toe. Of course, the strike dissipated, but it has left its mark.

The Una strike was a strike in the sense of the history of the working-class strike that happened from Chicago to Shanghai to Mumbai, but it was also a strike with a difference. It was a strike in the material as well as spiritual domains. It was against the working condition in which the workers feared for their lives. In the name of cows, they can be lynched anytime. It was also against religious sanctions. The strike was not only about the ceasing of work but also an act of defilement of the sacred order that sustains the oppression.

It would be difficult to find out the history of the first strike in India. Such history would be merely a claim. But we can be assured that it must have happened countless times in the past. If not history, it is good to have an allegory. The Indian dramaturgical text, the *Natyashastra*, talks about a strike. It says that Asuras were unhappy with their representation in the first-ever play, *Samundramanthan* (Churning of the Sea). They didn't like their humiliating representation. They complained to God, but their plea was not heard. They went on strike. They ceased movement; they paralyzed the performance by freezing the actors and paralyzing their memory. With the cessation of memory and movement, the actors failed to perform their acts. I read this powerful allegory as a siege of a humiliating performance.[13] The strike against humiliating representation is one of the most fundamental strikes in a caste world of representation.

---

[13] Brahma Prakash, *Cultural Labour: Conceptualizing the 'Folk Performance' in India* (New Delhi: Oxford University Press, 2019), 23–24.

The Strike that Ceased

The Indian authorities encountered a series of protests and strikes after the authoritarian regime came to power in 2014. But the Una Strike remains unique. It remains exceptional in its deployment of bodies, gestures, and artworks. By refusing to work and perform the assigned task, it sent a shockwave to the Hindu social order. *What will happen to us if they do not work for us?* No other protest movement in recent history in India has shaken the caste order at this level.

In 2016, India witnessed an unparalleled strike in Gujarat. The province is Gandhi's birthplace, but is also known as Hindutva's laboratory. The strike's background was the flogging of Dalit youths in public. On 11 July 2016, a cow vigilante group led by the upper caste attacked Dalit youths in the small town of Una, about 346 kilometres from the state capital city of Ahmedabad. The group accused them of cow slaughtering. The vigilante members kidnapped four of them and brought them to Una town. They took off their shirts, tied them to a car, and flogged them in broad daylight. The victims pleaded with folded hands. Their shoulders wore no sacred threads, but their bodies got bloody marks. It was the open, bare body in submission. The violence did not stop there. The vigilantes recorded the violent act and shared it on social media. It was a display of bravado mixed with upper-caste snobbery and supremacist pride. It was the fun of violence. It was years of silence. It was an act of lynching. It was a sadistic pleasure. The vigilantes indeed had violent fun!

The event took a new turn when Dalit activists encountered the video. They felt agitated. They decided to mobilize the communities. They called upon the communities to come out and end this daily humiliation. They fused their anger using newly acquired social media platforms. Whatever they could find: WhatsApp, Facebook, and other sharing platforms. As the flogging video went viral with the agitating messages of the activists, it created an uproar. Though the communities faced humiliation daily, it came as a tipping point. Martin Macwan, then the director of the Navsarjan Trust, an organization working on caste issues, had a point:

> Stories and photographs never had any impact, but the videos that the gloating *gau rakshaks* uploaded via social media went viral. Every Dalit village, not just in Gujarat but [also] all over India, could see these young boys being brutally thrashed. People said, 'the mob is using police *dandas* in broad daylight in an open place. The cops were standing around laughing, giving their *lathis* to be used. The men used vile, filthy abuse. It was sickening to watch.' Our people have had enough. The youth especially is livid. They are filled with violent anger.[14]

The older generations' responses were still very cold, but the young felt enraged when they saw the clip. They saw it again and again. Knowing that they were seeing their own bodies and humiliation, they watched it to understand their own social position. As they watched, they felt flogged. The anger was simmering; the internalized violence was being externalized. For some, the incident brought back old memories. Old memories felt not that old. It was live on the streets. How to stop it? Strike!

On 18 July 2016, Dalits in several parts of Gujarat took to the streets. They stopped traffic and disrupted daily life. Many parts of Gujarat witnessed a total strike. Angry protestors damaged government property. They clashed with the police and set fire to government buildings. It was a showdown against the caste show.

Another similar protest happened on 2 April 2018 when the Supreme Court tried to dilute the SCs/STs (Prevention of Atrocities) Act. To protest, Dalit organizations called a *Bharat bandh* (all-India strike). The *Bharat bandh* turned into a big event.

---

[14] Mari Marcel Thekaekara, 'The Dalit Fightback at Una is India's Rosa Parks Moment', *The Wire*, 13 August 2016, https://thewire.in/rights/the-dalit-fightback-at-una-is-indias-rosa-parks-moment

Not known that way, but it was one of the biggest one-day strikes in recent history. The massive protest brought India to a standstill. Both strikes were an attempt to lay down the siege of the incessant cease of caste society. It was similar to the shutting of a factory by workers in a conventional sense.

The Una strike took another interesting turn when the umbrella organization asked the Dalit community members to stop cleaning work. *Stop picking up garbage, stop picking up carcasses. Let the sewer flow in the cities, let the sewage flow in the houses, and let Hindu society clean its own dirt and shit.* As garbage started piling on the roads and the sewers of the cities started choking, Hindu society was in shock. Against the constant economic and social blockade of the lower castes, it was the lower castes' blockade of the upper caste. The sewer was blocked. The gutter was blocked. From latrines to bathrooms, from the kitchen to the garden, the blockades were everywhere. Within days, the strike entered from house to house, from the kitchen to the garbage bin. Decomposed bodies, plastic bags, fouled air, and sacred cows lying dead in the dirt. Pure and impure, dead and alive, sacred and profane came together.

In direct action, the protesters participated in a series of acts. They refused to collect and dispose of the garbage. Instead of disposing them at the designated places, they started dumping them at government offices and public spaces. Strikers would come in trucks and trolleys with loads of carcasses. They would dump them at civil offices. They would defy, they would defile, and they would register their anger and go. The slogan was too apt: *Tumhari amma, tum karo antim sanskar* ('Your mother, you perform the last rites)'. It was a slogan to withdraw from caste service and ritual obligations.

'Violent' Gestures of Non-violent Protest

While we tend to see civil society protests as logical and peaceful, protests such as the Una Strike and the *Bharat bandh* are usually seen as emotional outbursts of the communities. Their body posits a case of what scholars call an agitated irrationality. They don't seem to maintain control over their bodies and emotions.

They cry, they curse, they shout, they get agitated. They don't follow the assigned paths. They deviate from the routes recommended by the cops. They behave like 'rioters'. They don't appear to have learnt any lessons in the choreography of protest. They don't get time to rehearse before coming to the protest. They are not organized. Organizations don't have command over them. They march on the call, in anger, in sadness, for what they feel was an injustice. They come out to the streets to show that they are there, in bodies and spirits. We see a sea of angry eyes, but it is difficult to discern a singular gesture. Are they carrying symbols or physical actions?

The dance scholar Susan Leigh Foster, says that the body and the symbol cannot be separated. In her view, a body always carries a vast reservoir of signs and symbols.[15] So even if one participates in physical actions, one carries the signs. But how do we read the gestures that do not seem to find clear articulation? Hands are rising but in multiple directions. People are marching but with many diversions. Neither their bodies are synchronized nor their actions. Actions are not yet formed. Organizations are still in formation. The march remains dispersed; the movements indiscernible. But something is happening there. That's important. Songs are trying to find an audience; slogans are in search of resonance; bodies are looking for alliances. Assembly is dispersed before it has arrived. Solidarity is still a distant dream. Caste society is so senseless that solidarity has not yet been born. They are marching alone. Rarely do others join them. Like the BLM, even with the fake tears, no one has come to say that we are sorry for the wrong.

Protestors are out in the streets. They are blocking the roads. They are laying siege. Their numbers are not that big. When they

---

[15] Susan Leigh Foster, 'Choreographies of Protest', *Theatre Journal*, Vol.55, no.3 (2003): 395–412.

go to shut down, they are chased away by the police and crowds. But then the question comes: how do the protestors come together without a choreography of protest? They are marching with people alone, with their own people having similar experiences. They are the so-called Untouchables, marginalized, and a small section of Muslim minorities. Their concerns are connected with the cows. They are bodies that can be lynched. It was the call of a general strike that brought them together. A general strike, in Joshua Clover's words, 'unifies the experience of quotidian miseries'. It shows them (the protestors) the 'fragmentary glimpses of something beyond them'. It allows the individual (worker) an intuition of the world toward which revolution strives.[16]

Unlike other peaceful modes of protests, the Una Strike was not about a gesture of plea. It was not about the petition. It was not about submission and surrender. They had not come to kneel. They had not come to sit-in. One is not saying that those gestures are not powerful. One is fundamentally saying that these gestures do not work for them. *You can't surrender when you are subsumed.* You won't plead when you know that your pleas don't work. You submit; that is what they want. Protestors knew that unless they showed their anger, the authorities would not talk to them. In fact, it would become another act of humiliation. What they were asking for was the right to equality. It is a right. It cannot be pleaded. Some of them are enshrined in the Constitution. Some of them they wanted to take. The point is that you cannot surrender further after you have folded your hands.

The act of taking the knee would be read as an act of surrender. Submission will only give further courage to upper castes. This is ultimately what caste society expects from the low castes. *Kneel down if you see they are coming. Bow down in their honour.* The symbols of surrender have failed to engender resistance.

From the language of submission and victimhood, one needs

---

[16] Joshua Clover, *Riot. Strike. Riot: The New Era of Uprisings* (London: Verso Books, 2019), 140.

to move to the language of confrontation. The very idea of the so-called low castes ready to confront the so-called upper castes can create resistance. You do what the upper castes don't like: assertion, aspiration, articulation, loudness. When you use their language, they feel threatened. Of course, you can't become them, but you can produce the equality of emotions. You will break the stereotypical images in which they carry the caste hegemony. Such anger and violence are reserved for Kshatriyas and not for Dalits. Even the perceived violence of the Dalits is seen as a breach of contract. Resistance happens when one reverses this relationship.

Hindu society at large is not familiar with their assertive gestures. Reversing this image, angry Dalit youths marched with sticks and poles in their hands. The skinners who never said no to obligation applied for a gun licence in some areas.[17] The aim was not to enact violence but to show fits of anger and equality of emotion.

In the Una strike, the protestors' grievances were against the authorities. It was not the upper castes but the state that signed the contract to save their rights. The state was breaching the contract; therefore, this breach was important. It was a breach of contract of services against the breach of the state.

Gestures in the Una strike were full of performative violence. It was about how we won't *tolerate it any longer*. But what would they do? They didn't have the power to enact similar violence. They engaged in performative violence. It was physical but also symbolic. Jeffrey S. Juris defines it as a specific mode of communication through which activists seek to produce social transformation by staging 'symbolic rituals of confrontation'.[18] Every day protests by marginalized groups, Dalits, Adivasis, nomadic communities

---

[17] H.L. Dusadh, 'Needed: Licensed Weapons to Boost the Moral of Dalits', *Forward Press*, 2 August 2016, https://www.forwardpress.in/2016/08/needed-licensed-weapons-to-boost-the-morale-of-dalits/

[18] J.S. Juris, 'Violence Performed and Imagined Militant: Action, the Black Bloc and the Mass Media in Genoa', *Critique of Anthropology* 25, no. 4 (2005): 413.

in India go unnoticed, but damaging government property and blocking roads gives them the 'required' media attention. The Una strike was not reported by the mainstream media until it turned 'violent'. The mainstream media termed it a riot. They were biased, but they were not entirely wrong. There are cases of protest violence that can be termed 'irrational'. Protestors blocked the road and ran into a riot-like situation.

The performative violence was intended to create a problem. Slavoj Žižek says that the aim of such violence is 'to signal that they were a problem that they could no longer be ignored'.[19] If the Dalits could have organized a non-violent vigil, all they would have got was small coverage in the media or not even that. Though the gestures cannot be captured, they cannot be termed random or senseless. Unfinished gestures are responses to the specific economy of signification. It does not come through rehearsed bodies but through the mnemonic reservoirs that connect history, experience, and the present.

While Dalit protestors avoid violent recourse, they remain critical of the Gandhian mode of protest. There are popular sayings among them. *Hungry people cannot go on hunger strikes. You cannot show your vulnerable image that brings more traumas.* Ambedkar, too, wanted to create a positive image of the oppressed caste communities that embody internalized violence. He asked them to 'Educate, Agitate, Organize', instead of presenting and reproducing the same victimhood image. The Una strike was about agitation.

Agitation was doing two things together. It was stirring and shaking the conscience of the oppressed communities who had internalized violence. But agitation also aimed to expose the injustices of the upper caste. It was challenging them on moral grounds by sending them into a sense of guilt. That often does not work in a caste society. Ambedkar himself led a Mahad

---

[19] Slavoj Žižek, *Violence: Six Sideways Reflections* (New York: Picador, 2009), 77.

agitation. According to Shivasundar, he (Ambedkar) came to two conclusions: One cannot trigger a sense of guilt in the so-called upper castes through peaceful agitations because these castes do not think that caste practice is wrong. This is what happened. After Ambedkar led the Mahad *satyagraha*, instead of feeling ashamed, the upper-caste communities purified the tank with cow urine and cow dung.[20]

In the context of 'hands up, don't shoot', Anusha Kedhar shows a few ways of reading gestures. Habitus becomes an interesting entry point. She argues 'how young black men and women in the US learn this gesture of surrender and submission early on when dealing with police'.[21] But in the case of the Una strike, it is precisely by going against the habitus, going against the surrendering attitudes, that Dalits could produce the strike action. Otherwise, actions would end up becoming a stereotype or failing to work in that society. The point is to bring everyone out of their habitus, both the upper castes and the lower castes.

Kedhar asks, but what happens when protest becomes a failed sign? 'When the bodily act of submission is not seen or heard?' In India, such signs work for civil society members but not for Dalits and other marginalized protestors. This also shows how some modes of protest and strike stick to one community and do not work for others. In the case of 'hands up, don't shoot', we see a formation of a new collective also coming from the white as well as other coloured communities. That moment has not yet arrived in the case of Dalit protestors in India, with a few exceptions. Rohith Vemula's death protest brought wider civil society groups led by students and youths. Usually, this does not happen. It is so

---

[20] 'Mahad Agitation India's First Civil Rights Movement', *The Hindu*, 20 March 2022. https://www.thehindu.com/news/national/karnataka/mahad-agitation-indias-first-civil-rights-movement/article65243499.ece?homepage=true

[21] Anusha Kedhar. "'Hands Up! Don't Shoot!": Gesture, Choreography, and Protest in Ferguson', *The Feminist Wire*, October 6 2014. https://www.thefeministwire.com/2014/10/protest-in-ferguson/

evident. How many civil society groups in Delhi engage with the 'Stop Killing Us' campaign of the Safai Karmachari Andolan that is working to end the practice of manual scavenging? Or can we say that civil society participates in protest action on their own conditions, only with a vulnerable body and not with an assertive body. It has also happened with minority protests in many parts of India.

Scholars offer a defensive argument, perhaps, to prove that they were not 'the irrational bodies'. They were not irrational. Kedhar notes that the actions of the protestors were carefully rehearsed and choreographed. The questions we can raise are what if they are not choreographed? What if they were unpredictable? What if they were not following the assigned paths? Does that make a protest unethical? Do they have the right to protest beyond the choreopoliced state? It is in this situation that civil society usually backtracks its support and often terms such protests as riots. But this is exactly the moment when protests chart out a new path. This diversion is not an error; it could not have been planned and propagated. This is what Rosa Luxemburg would like to see as 'eventuality'.[22]

> If, therefore, the Russian Revolution teaches us anything, it teaches above all that mass strike is not artificially 'made,' not 'decided' at random, not 'propagated,' but that it is a historical phenomenon which at a given moment, results from social conditions with historical inevitability.[23]

The dance scholar, André Lepecki, argues that if to be political is the ability to move freely, then the ideal political subject is the 'dancer'.[24] But in a neoliberal regime, a dancer is also a model of

---

[22] Joshua Clover, *Riot. Strike. Riot*, 143.

[23] Luxemburg, *The Mass Strike*.

[24] André Lepecki, 'Choreopolice and Choreopolitics: Or, the task of the dancer', *The Drama Review*, 57, no. 4 (2013): 13-27.

perfection and regimentation — an embodiment of skills and speeds. The dancer's body is the most appropriate and predictable body after a 'miss beauty' that a regime looks for disposal. Radical politics does not necessarily lie in the regime of the free flow of movement (like the free flow of capital) but in the most unpredictable 'moves'. Such moves bring newness as well as danger. It brings us signs that cannot be named, gestures that cannot be captured. It engenders a protest that can or cannot be choreographed but cannot be choreopoliced. It exists as a pose that can be named a strike.

When Strike Becomes an Artwork

Yates McKee, in his work *Strike Art*, asks: what is the relationship of art to the practice of radical politics today?[25] In a strike, we can see an artistic-oriented direct action bringing bodies in encounters with barricades. Recent protests show that the distance between the art work and protest work is vanishing, as are the dimensions of politics and aesthetics.

Some of the most animated art and poetry happens at the protest sites, during the strikes, and at the sites of occupation. If songs were the heart of the farmers' protest, poetry was the soul of Shaheen Bagh. While theatres, museums, and art galleries remained closed during the pandemic, we saw artists and singers coming to the assembly. More artwork happened at the protest sites; more theatre happened at the borders. More exhibitions came to the roads than the museums and national parades. Remember the beautiful trollies of the farmers' protest; remember the artwork at Shaheen Bagh.

Artists and writers were joining the protests and changing the site into an art space on the one hand. And on the other, protestors themselves were turning to artistic expressions. The Rohith Vemula protesters created powerful art. They turned the university

---

[25] Yates McKee, *Strike Art: Contemporary Art and the Post-Occupy Condition* (London: Verso, 2017), 1.

into *velivada* (caste village). Women at Shaheen Bagh turned the stage into storytelling. They had so many stories to share — stories they had not shared for years. Women performers from Punjab came dancing and singing. Tamil Nadu farmers came with skulls and bones to play their theatrics against the neoliberal state. They were all turning to fundamental cultural expressions. Likewise, the Una protestors carried out a series of art strikes. The Una strike was full of innovations. It was challenging not only the politics but the very sense of religion and aesthetics. They used cow carcasses and garbage as art materials.

Protestors dumping carcasses in civic spaces and government offices can be seen as an attack of the invisible theatre. Instead of collecting the garbage and carcasses, they started scattering them in the open spaces. The repulsive art was creating ripples in society. As Dalits and the marginalized castes stopped picking up the garbage, the cities started witnessing horrible scenes. The fouled air was filling the public sphere. Disgusting scenes were emerging from the streets. The scene was striking at the sensorial and sacred levels. The art strike was an act of defiance and defilement together. It was opening the scenes that the public sphere keeps hiding. It was an art strike in the full sense: 'impure' and full of 'impropriety'. Against the culture of fear and silence, it was a show of courage and resistance.

The exhibition was spreading across the streets. Bovine carcasses littered the roads. The foul air was so overpowering that one could not have escaped it. The scene of decaying animals, open garbage, and overflowing sewers was terrifying. It was sublime. Amidst the filth, dogs and carrion were having their feast. They were eating and scattering the bones; they were piling skins; they were pulling out limbs of cows; they were divulging the intestines of the sacred cow. No such powerful exhibition has happened in recent history in any art gallery. No sensorium could match the evocation. The black curtain and white cube could not have held it. In one stroke, Una exposed Hinduism, nationalism, and the Indian labouring castes' working condition. Una exposed the sacredness of the Hindu social order. Hindus were feeling helpless.

The protestors laughed at the helplessness of the Hindus who could not clean their own shit. They could not bury their own cow mothers. Nathubhai Parmar, social worker with the Dalit rights organisation Navsarjan, who was instrumental in organizing the art acts, was seeing and laughing. His eyes were filled with laughter: 'We were fed up. They call the cow their mother, so we decided: Let them look after their mothers.' The activist said, 'We put 20–30 dead cows into a truck and unloaded them in front of the collectors' office. Here, take your mother and bury her'.[26] The stink of rotting carcasses brought home the role Dalits play in society. The protestors also brought posters. They pasted them across the cities. Posters asked what independence meant for Dalits. It had the answer. Dalit youths getting flogged.

The art strike also brought another powerful exposition. It was positioned against the neoliberal state's image-building and performance indexes project. If caste society relies on imitation, the neoliberal regime relies on permutation — the order of the arrangement to hype the number. The authoritarian regime was more interested in image-building. Critics pointed out how 'Vibrant Gujarat' was an organized performance. It was choreographed by the lobbying company APCO Worldwide, the second-largest independent PR and lobbying firm known for campaigning for leaders, dictators, and global investors.[27]

Christophe Jaffrelot noted that Modi understood the importance of image-making. He hired the media to agitate Hindu communities.[28] That resulted in the worst form of rioting

---

[26] Shoaib Daniyal, "'Your Mother, You Take Care of it': Meet the Dalits behind Gujarat's Stirring Cow Carcass Protests', *Scroll.in*, 23 July 2016, https://scroll.in/article/812329/your-mother-you-take-care-of-it-meet-the-dalits-behind-gujarats-stirring-cow-carcass-protests

[27] Christophe Jaffrelot, 'Narendra Modi and the power of television in Gujarat'. *Television & New Media*, Vol. 16, no. 4 (2015), 346–353.

[28] Jaffrelot, 'Narendra Modi and the power of television in Gujarat'.

in Gujarat in 2002. Televisions telecast the burned bodies from Godhra with the promise of Modi that he would take a revenge. Modi emerged as the darling of Hindutva. Jean Dreze calls it a 'spruced up image'.[29] It was not the substance but the spruced-up image that was creating performance. In a climactic moment, a street in Guangzhou, China, was straightaway photoshopped as a street in Ahmedabad.

The Una protestors troubled these image-building and performance indexes. Activists started photoshopping images from 'Vibrant Gujarat'. They picked up the promotional aid of the Gujarat Tourism Department. In the image, Amitabh Bachchan, the Bollywood actor, is asking tourists to come to Gujarat to experience *khushbu Gujarat ki* (the scent of Gujarat).

In a strike, Dalit activists altered the image and words with Bachchan standing with cow carcasses in the background. He can be seen welcoming tourists to come to experience *badbu Gujarat ki* (the stink of Gujarat). They also made postcards out of those images and sent them to big personalities to experience the stink. The caption read: *Photoshop hame bhi aati hai* (we also know how to photoshop). The art strike thoroughly exposed the 'Vibrant Gujarat' model. It worked as a counter-performance. It offered a powerful critique of the performance regime. It gave birth to a new art form in which activists such as Nathubhai Parmar put up permanent artwork in which he installed a cow prototype with its stomach exposed and intestine choked with plastic. He hung fluid-soaked plastic taken out from the real cow on an everyday basis. Even after the Una strike, he would show how 70–80 kilograms of plastic are removed from the intestine of just one cow. It was another exposition that, too, was striking.[30]

The Una strike could not sustain for a long time. It was not

[29] Jean Dreze, 'The Gujarat Muddle.' *The Hindu*, April 11, 2014.

[30] Ashish Chauhan, 'Ex-Cow Skinner Gets under the Skin of Cows to Save Them', *The Times of India*, 8 May 2018, https://timesofindia.indiatimes.com/city/ahmedabad/ex-cow-skinner-gets-under-the-skin-of-cows-to-save-them/articleshow/64071822.cms

planned. The protestors were daily wage labourers. But they sent a red signal to the local authorities and the Hindu social order. The strike struck at the social, corporeal, political as well as the physic levels. It created a gutsy, filthy, and unsettling response. It reclaimed the idea of a strike. It expanded its definition in cultural spheres. It will keep asking us, if there is caste and if there is exploitation, why can't we strike.

8. A Show for the Dead

Death, Mourning, and Solidarity

> *Our mourning, our letting ourselves grieve over the loss of loved ones is an expression of our commitment, a form of communication and communion.*
>
> — bell hooks[1]

It is said about the young Siddhartha that he was so privileged that he had no idea about the suffering of the poor, the sick, and the aged. He did not know that a human being also dies. He was at a loss when he saw people grieving for the dead. He was in shock when he saw people mourning on the streets. His encounter with death and mourning changed the meaning and purpose of his life. It was the sense of vulnerability that brought Buddhism as a religion into this world. It was compassion and interdependence that could make this human solidarity possible. It is another matter that Buddhism tends to depoliticize the question of vulnerability by accepting it as a human condition and a fact of life. The point that has to be made is that mourning and vulnerability are not always a low point. When exposed to adversity, we often find our deepest courage, strength and solidarity.

Perhaps we have seen the death and loss of our near and dear ones. Some more, some less. I have grieved so much in my life that I feel dread. After every loss, I decided I would not cry any longer. I will turn into a stone, I will not grieve anymore. Once you have

---

[1] bell hooks, *All About Love* (New York: HarperCollins, 2000), 201.

witnessed the extreme, it seems as if you might lose the capacity to grieve and mourn again. But this does not happen. Every time you try to stop, the eyes sprinkle tears like springs. How do these eyes hold so much water? Every new loss brings the sea, the wave that shakes the body, the weight on which we get carried like a ferry on the sea. Touch consoles us, but it also brings more tears.

Mourning is not necessarily an exterior emotion as it often appears. It is a movement that comes from within. It is the inside that pours out like a volcanic eruption when it comes out from the fissures as fires. The body becomes so porous that it becomes all breath. It becomes all wax and melts like a candle. It is perhaps the most therapeutic and cathartic act of human life. It shows how much pain one might have been holding. It reiterates that our capacity to grieve cannot be exhausted.

What else can you cut after you have slashed the tongue? What else can you curtail once you have curtailed life and breath? What could be the most extreme case of curtailment? What could be the most excessive idea of control? Can we still affirm the politics of life?

My intention here is not to ask the *yaksha prashnas* that Yaksha had asked Yudhisthira in the Mahabharata. When Yaksha asked Yudhisthira what the most puzzling thing in the world was, he said that every day one sees countless living entities dying, but one still acts and thinks as if one will live forever. It would be trivializing to ask such questions. It would be a case of justifying crimes against humanity and the genocide committed by authoritarian regimes. I am asking the bare minimum questions. Perhaps we all ask these questions in extreme situations of despair, in the condition of breathlessness, in situations where we have almost given up on our struggle to stand up. However, as ardent and adamant adherents of life and freedom, we ask these questions even after death. 'What can you do to me now?'. It reminds us of the song by Willie Nelson, the American country musician,

What can you do to me now?
That you haven't done to me already
You broke my pride and made me cry out loud
What can you do to me now

I'm seeing things that I never thought I'd see
You've opened up the eyes inside of me
How long have you been doing this to me
I'm seeing sides of me that I can't believe.[2]

When humanity is at stake, these questions relate to the politics of life and death. When the last refuge of humanity — grieving — itself is perceived as a threat. The one who grieves is placed under surveillance. The authorities deploy a microscope to decipher the colour of tears. It checks and grades the shades of sorrow that can turn anytime into a sea of rage. One is not allowed to mourn; one is not allowed to weep aloud; one is not allowed to have a dignified mourning and death. One is not allowed to become part of the bodies and alliances from which one is born.

A saying goes that an unfulfilled mourning, an interrupted grieving, an unnatural death, and injustice — all haunt. Yes, it haunts … it haunts. It ensures that power can parade its prowess, but it cannot be at peace.

One can understand a situation in which a power is afraid of protest and subversion; if it is fearful of questions and criticisms, or it is terrified of truth and dialogue. Why does it have to be afraid of mourning and grieving? What does it find alarming in a wailing sound? What does it find dangerous in a ritual that itself is called the last ritual?

This essay is about the concerns that connect us to mourning and its curtailment by an authoritarian regime. It connects us at the brink of humanity. What remains buried in mourning

---

[2] Willie Nelson And Family, 'What Can You Do to Me Now', YouTube, 9 February 2017, https://www.youtube.com/watch?v=wgEdjlamxbg

and grieving, that power is so afraid of, is how mourning — the moment of vulnerability — becomes invulnerable in its most precarious moment. If an authority is so insecure about these acts, we know that mourning does something. It has something hidden within it. One way of seeing grieving is that it is not about loss but about what remains with us; the experiences, the memories, the touch, the regret, and the acts that colour the meaning of our life.

From Kashmir to Telangana, to Delhi and Uttar Pradesh, Indian authorities have banned several mourning processions in the past. Of course, the people of Kashmir have witnessed this curtailment at an extreme level. Mourning was clamped down in the valley of Kashmir along with the cries for freedom. The body disappeared before the mourning could take place. The family keeps waiting for the dead. The grave keeps waiting for the body. The tombstone of the empty grave of Maqbool Bhat, the founder of the Jammu and Kashmir Liberation Front (JKLF), still reads, 'this grave waits for him'.[3] The mourning that was a passing moment has become a looming wait. It dwells in the valleys and the landscape of Kashmir. It soars like a cloud messenger. It cries with the river and the rain. Have you heard how the River Jhelum cries in the song of Faheem Abdullah, '*Jhelam roya*' (Jhelum cried)?[4]

Jhelum cried, Jhelum cried
For the sake of Kashmir
Everyone has died,
Everyone has died,
but the ones who live on cry for they die (everyday).

The river cries but carries the message of freedom and curtailment. It says that when mourning is not allowed, it becomes

[3] Maqbool Bhat was considered the architect of the Kashmiri freedom struggle. He was hanged at New Delhi's infamous Tihar Jail on 11 February 1984, and buried in the jail complex.

[4] Faheem Abdullah, '*Jhelum Roya*', https://kasheer.net/lyrics/jhelum-mad-in-kashmir-rauhan-malik-faheem-abdullah/

enduring. It is not going to die before it accomplishes its task, before it departs the soul, before it buries the body with full dignity.

For many years now, Kashmir has been the Indian laboratory of curtailment. It comes in various forms: bans, blackouts, blockades, lockdowns, curfews, clampdowns, crackdowns, shutdowns, shootdowns, barricading, and so on. The forms of curtailment are first practised in the valley before they reach the mainland. Not to be denied or delayed, they reach, maybe not with the same severity or in the same forms, but they reach. It was not surprising that the Kashmir model of clamping down on mourning and procession soon became a reality in other parts of India. The Hathras rape case of 2020 in Uttar Pradesh, in which upper-caste men raped and killed a Dalit woman, is a poignant example of this case. I will discuss it in detail to explore the power of mourning and why the state wants to curtail it.

The question we should also ask is what is it that we are mourning: are we mourning the loss of an individual life or are we mourning our collective failure? Are we trying to see death in isolation and fatalism, or are we also mourning our democracy and justice systems? Shall we also mourn these institutions, or shall we say that they have lost their moral right to be mourned? Are we mourning and giving up space to authority for its spectacle, or are we mourning and sharing our grief to make it the point of living? We can ask many such questions.

For all these reasons, neither all assembly nor all mourning can be equally valued. We see how the state orchestrates the mourning of an army jawan with full state ceremonies. We have seen how authority loves to sermonize sacrifice and mourning. It waits for the dead body like a vulture waiting for a grand feast. Mourning becomes the 'real' celebration of the nation after every death of an army person. Yet the very same authority remains afraid of egalitarian mourning. It does not allow the mourning of a rape victim or a caste victim. It also depends on who mourns against whom. One cannot mourn against an immoral authority. Still, against a moral authority, mourning becomes a moral complaint. In the case of authoritarianism, the same mourning becomes an act of resistance. While feeling an extreme sense of isolation, mourning turns into a demonstration of the collective.

The coronavirus pandemic brought a situation in which people were forced to grieve in isolation. It provided a rationale for the state to insulate people from their sense of belonging. The reason given was to stop the spread of the virus, but its consequences were far-reaching. Isolated grieving tends to individualize every death. It sees it as a personal loss. It was unsurprising that the authorities hid and clamped down on Covid-19 deaths. They removed the shrouds from the dead bodies to expunge the evidence.[5] The state feared that the mourning could erupt in protest at any time. It tried all possible ways to contain and curtail them.

Sometimes, it is only through such bans and curtailment that we can understand the significance of mourning. Then mourning becomes more intense and grieving more meaningful. Mourning from a ritual act suddenly becomes a political act that leads to the birth of a new subject. Such mourning expands the canvas of memory, rich in details and layered with meanings; mobilizing every limb of our bodies, one enters into a trance and has a dialogue with the dead.

Ideally, the state should have taken responsibility in the background of the mass Covid-19 deaths. Ideally, the state should have mourned the deaths, lowering the unwavering flag of the idealized nation, lowering the tone of its high pitch slogan. Ideally, it should have facilitated the mourning as it does after a soldier's death on the borders, but these are all only ideals amidst horrid tales. We cannot expect a 'necropolitical' state that sponsors death

---

[5] Omar Rashid, 'Shrouds Removed from Bodies Buried in Sand on Ganga Ghats: Probe Ordered', *The Hindu*, 26 May 2021, https://www.thehindu.com/news/national/other-states/shrouds-removed-from-graves-along-ganga-in-prayagraj/article34645290.ece

to mourn the dead, grieve for the mass deaths, and offer healing to the people who have suffered.[6] One does not expect the state and authorities to participate in egalitarian mourning. Still, one expects that some sense may prevail.

Egalitarian mourning, as Judith Butler says, is about the possibility of expanding 'the very conception of the human'.[7] It brings an extreme sense of vulnerability, as well as the human capacity for suffering and healing. That moment shows how much we can take, how much we can possess. What happens when mourning is curtailed? What grief does inside, mourning does outside. It gives emotion a physicality, a face, a force, and movement to fly with the dead.

The right to have dignity in death is perhaps one of the last virtues of humanity. It is the last act of caring. It is expected that no one should expect unexpected grief, and no one should live the life of a dead person. No one should face indignity in death. One does not want the dead to be dishonoured and a life to be curtailed at this level when one lives between life and death. No one would like to see the walking dead carrying their own corpses for disposal.

But we must remember that this is the power of 'liberal' democracies. It is here, resting on its founding violence of dispossession, exploitation, and extraction. It can give death and withhold death as the sovereign rite of regulating life. Achille Mbembe says that this 'necropower' is exercised not only through spectacular forms of terror but also by inflicting 'small doses' of death on people living 'at the edge of life'.[8] Death with indignity can be perceived as small doses of death.

---

[6] Extending Foucault's idea, Achille Mbembe describes the necropolitical state as a state that does not only hold the right to kill but also the right to expose people to death. Achille Mbembe, 'Necropolitics', *Foucault in an Age of Terror* (London: Palgrave MacMillan, 2008), 152–182.

[7] Judith Butler, 'Violence, Mourning, Politics', *Studies in Gender and Sexuality* 4, no. 1 (2003): 9–37.

[8] Mbembe, 'Necropolitics', 152–182.

Death and Indignity

The second wave of the pandemic in India brought death, destruction, and despair at an unimaginable scale. Death and indignity spread to the streets. As people kept hiding in their homes, or in hideouts, the street became a site to behold. The street turned into a theatre — an epic theatre — of our times. It made things visible in the vilest ways. While indignity unfolded on the streets, mourning could not find its place. At least mourning could have repented for the apathy that filled us with indignity.

Despite its actual physical absence, mourning became the ambience of the day and night. It was looming at large, along with the fear of the virus. It was something that one could not have held together in the absence of the collective, in isolation. Life was cut short, breath was cut short, grieving was cut in half, and mourning was cut short completely. Humanity was peeled from its own body in moments and layers like an onion.

While death itself was unbearable, death with indignity is a burden that will be carried in our memories of the pandemic in the future. What would we remember when we remember Covid-19? Naked bodies lying on the streets; the authorities removing the shrouds from the dead; the image of a woman supplying air to her gasping husband in an auto; un-cremated corpses — lying in wait for a pyre — kept in bags and concealed because of the fear of contamination. These have become the defining images of the Covid-19 pandemic.

What could be a worse feeling than to feel we have failed the dying? We could not provide them with flowers, incense, and firewood. Thus, the spectral utterance against authority, 'what can you do to me now' (I am dead), doesn't work. It causes indignity even in death. It kills the dead. It enslaves hope in a dream. It can curtail mourning. Pragya Tiwari's report sums up these indignities:

Dead bodies of coronavirus patients are left unattended on

hospital floors, corridors, or even under hospital beds —
naked. Others lie in mortuaries for days and arrive stacked
up in hearses before they are cremated. In one case, the dead
body of a man suspected to have died of COVID-19 was taken
for post mortem in a garbage truck, and in another, health
workers were caught on video dumping a corpse in an open
ditch. In one of the most horrifying cases to come to light,
the dead body of an 82-year-old woman who died from the
virus lay rotting for eight days in a toilet cubicle in the hospital
where she was being treated before being discovered.[9]

Such treatment of the dead shows the end of humanity. But it
also brings the body and thinking to the edge, on the barricades.
In the absence of collectivity and solidarity, mourning spread on
faces like makeup on corpses. It could not hold you; it did not cry
with you. It did not lend you a shoulder. The tears dried in the
eyes; feelings, in the heart. Humanity lost its sense in the absence
of touch. Not allowed to speak to their neighbours, the walls were
wailing without a sound.

What could be a more heart-wrenching scene than crying
but not being able to touch and calm each other? You could not
hold their hand; you couldn't press their fingers. You couldn't
hug. You couldn't lean on the body of your beloved. You couldn't
kiss the head of the dead. Families were falling in their own eyes
after failing to give a dignified departure to the dead. Gary B.B.
Coleman was still singing in the distance:

The sky is crying
Can you see the tears roll down the streets
I've been looking for my baby

---

[9] Pragya Tiwari, 'Indians Have Only Themselves to Blame for the
Health Disaster', *Al Jazeera*, 5 July 2020. https://www.aljazeera.com/
opinions/2020/7/5/indians-have-only-themselves-to-blame-for-the-health-
disaster

And I've been wondering where can she be.[10]

In this situation of unspeakable hell, some locations were speaking too loudly. Those sites were turning into scenarios. In the absence of documents, they carried the collective memory of the catastrophe. The first scenario was emerging from hospitals where patients were dying without oxygen. The second scenario was emerging from crematoriums. There were bodies and fire all around. The one who survived was burning in anger and grief, and the one who was dead was burning without wood. One body was coming after another as there was no end to it. Bodies were spilling out from the graveyard, crematoriums were falling short, firewood was getting over, and iron furnaces were melting like hearts. The cities were under lockdown, and the corpses had jammed the crematorium. Though the scenes came from the pandemic, they were also scenarios of curtailment. It also says that the necropolitical state can bring a pandemic any day by exposing people to death. The third scenario was emerging from the banks of the rivers in North India, where dead bodies were floating like dead fishes on the surface. They spread for miles. Reuters shot an image of the dead bodies lying on the banks of the rivers. It showed hundreds of bodies, covered with saffron cloth, spread for miles.

Separated by bamboo sticks, the bodies looked like artwork — the bodywork of the fascists. Before we move on to understanding why mourning was banned, let us discuss the political and cultural apathy on the question of what exactly has to be mourned.

A Crime Against Humanity

The second wave of the pandemic left millions dead. Millions stood aghast: helpless, horrified, and humiliated. Who would have thought that a crime against humanity could be organized in such a cool and composed manner? Who would have thought that a

---

[10] Gary B.B. Coleman, 'The Sky is Crying', YouTube, 18 April 2017, https://www.youtube.com/watch?v=71Gt46aX9Z4

crime against humanity could be managed in such a magnanimous way that the nation's monument and the bodies of the masses would be in a mound together in this brand new India?

When the roads were empty, and the cities were turning into ghost towns, the rivers and drains were floating with bodies as dead fish float on ponds after being poisoned. The dead were silently walking in the dark and sealing their bodies in the sand so that the nation's image would not be sullied. Death and destruction were expected in the pandemic, but not the humanitarian crisis of exodus that unfolded in front of us. The tragedy was expected, but not the nakedness. The meaning of life and death became meaningless, and the Aristotelian tragedy lost its plot against the Indian authoritarian ploy as neither the nation nor the king was ready to mourn, and the chorus kept singing the king's praises.

How many deaths will you count? How many deaths will you mourn? How many bodies will you bury? And how many bodies will you burn? Not one, or ten, but millions have died. While the sources remain mum, some said one million. Some said five million. Some said more. We will never know the numbers. The leader said that it was the invisible enemy. It seems, therefore, that death has to be invisible or invisibilized. The number is true to the spirit of a crime against humanity or a genocide. A genocide becomes genocidal in a true sense when we cannot count the number of deaths; when bodies pile on bodies; when bodies lay in potholes; when the dead appear from everywhere like ghosts; when bodies disappear from everywhere like the Holocaust; when the dead fill the mortuaries; when the dead fall from the ambulances as signs of a last protest; when the dead lose not only life, but also their dignity in the end. We cannot describe it in any other way but as a genocide and a crime against humanity.

We know the stories of the Holocaust. How many dead were paid their last respects during the Holocaust? Even after the deaths, bodies were purged. Bone crushers were used to turn the bodies into dust. Ashes were thrown into the rivers. Historians count the bones, not the dust that the bodies flew away. The Indian state was perfecting genocide in its gory details. By removing the shrouds from the bodies, they performed a genocide in both letter and spirit.

Genocide is the dead end of the body, its spaces, and its possibilities. It is the name of infinite atrocities. It is the number that cannot be counted. It is a loss that cannot be surmounted. It is about the deaths that cannot be solemnized. Tears dry; you cannot cry. Your eyes work like a camera lucida. They see. They cease. They sketch with accuracy. Life becomes an archive.

The real casualty was not happening in emergency wards but in the casual response of the authoritarian state. The state remained relaxed as if nothing had happened. There was no sense of remorse. There was no acknowledgement of the mass deaths. The message was clear: We don't care. We care for what we care for: image, power, perception, and elections. While people were fighting the pandemic, the state was fighting for its image and perception.

It is not enough to say that the state had not anticipated the spread. Do we really believe that the party and the system that could manage every booth in the elections could not arrange for beds? The party that could arrange for kerosene oil, LPG gas, and arsenals to carry out carnage could not arrange for oxygen cylinders. The party that could buy MLAs and MPs did not have money to buy vaccines. The prime minister of the nation, who could afford a luxurious plane, and could build a grand vista, didn't have money to vaccinate his citizens. Let us also accept that the government was unprepared to handle the pandemic, but it was never the nation's priority. Their priorities were set. The elections were coming. They will be out soon. Standing with you, arm in arm. They will create a spectacle, and you will forget your loss in the glory of the nation.

We have learnt that to organize a genocide, one does not need to build gas chambers or extermination camps. You do not need to send people into exile. Switch off the supply of oxygen and leave people gasping. The point is to suffocate them, make them gasp. It is economical. It is innovative. It is unblemished. You don't need firewood to burn the bodies. You don't let the fire stop. Bones will crackle the bones; bodies will burn the bodies. Let them die in agony, in a slow, agonizing, and humiliating death.

After the migrants' exodus, one anticipated that they would be left to die in an extreme situation. After the massacre of Muslims in the heart of the capital, it was confirmed that the minorities would be murdered at the will of the majority. And they will be blamed for their own deaths. Of course, the poor who cannot afford health facilities would die carrying the Ayushman Bharat card on their heads.[11] Nobody would have thought that the middle class and the Hindu upper castes — the nation's cheerleaders — would have the same fate. One did not expect that the divine citizens of the Hindu nation would beg for oxygen, and even the elites would die for want of ICU beds.

Irrespective of their positions, everyone learnt a lesson. Leaving aside the minorities who will be excluded from the National Register for the Citizens list, the very proud citizens were paraded for their health. They were all out like denizens in the dead of night. They were hapless, helpless, and half in their appearance and strengths. They were made vulnerable. Their sense of pride was taken away. Their self was shattered like a mirror falling from the wall of fame.

Who knows, they may feel more obliged to the nation now than they felt during the demonetization drive.[12] Who knew

---

[11] The Ministry of Health and Family Welfare claims that the Ayushman Bharat card will provide free access to health insurance coverage to low-income earners; however, independent critics find many loopholes in the scheme.

[12] In 2016, the government, in an abrupt declaration, announced the demonetization of banknotes of 500 and 1,000 currency notes. The decision,

Hannah Arendt's reading of fascism may come true again — the more people die, more legitimacy is conferred upon the Fuhrer as a strong leader. Totalitarianism's 'defiance of positive laws claims to be a higher form of legitimacy'.[13] It has happened before. The hope is that it is not repeated again and that genocide is not harvested like the riots.

Mourning Banned

In 2017, the Tajikistan government banned loud wailing and other excessively overt forms of mourning and black clothing at funerals.[14] They termed it as 'extravagant emotions'. As a part of this ban, loud wailing, hiring professional mourners at funeral services, and ritual practices like pulling hair in grief were banned. The authority also banned chasing after the coffin, loud ululation, and other related actions. Common Tajikistani citizens were surprised by the decision. 'What the hell! How can you ban mourning?' The state saw such mourning as a site of radicalization. Thus, it had to be banned.

Mourning, unlike grieving, is a collective expression. The collective show of mourning has been a common expression of grief in the Middle East and various regions of Asia and Africa. The practice was also quite prevelant among Chinese peasant societies. There is a sense of social solidarity in how grief and death are expressed in many traditional societies worldwide. Grappling with grief, in these societies, is not an individual act. There is the Igbo tradition, an African way of mourning. It is a 'performative, expressive outward mourning, where you take every call and you tell and retell the story of what happened', writes Chimamanda Ngozi Adichie in *Notes on Grief*.[15] In such societies, she says,

according to critics, adversely affected the Indian economy.

[13] Hannah Arendt, *The Origins of Totalitarianism* (London: Penguin, 2017).

[14] Maria Perez, 'Tajikistan Officials Forbid Loud Crying at Funerals', *Newsweek*, 26 September 2017, https://www.newsweek.com/tajikistan-funerals-religion-671536

[15] Chimamanda Ngozi Adichie, *Notes on Grief* (London: Fourth Estate,

'isolation is anathema', and 'stop crying' a refrain. Thus, mourning is the only way out.

It is the ultimate act of showing solidarity to the individual and family, who otherwise grieve in isolation. These practices may look absurd to some of us, but they can also be seen as one way of showing solidarity with the family and respect for the dead. It is also a show of dignity after death. Mourning is not just about grieving; it is also about a collective demonstration of grief. Mourning is a time when people share the life history of a person. Chasing after the coffin is about showing the dead how much we love them. It is about showing them that we have tried our best to bring you back or that we all wanted to come with you but were left behind. I remember participating in several such mourning ceremonies, which created extraordinary emotion. It creates an atmosphere of extreme grief and anguish. The whole atmosphere is mobilized as though the world is grieving. It becomes an extraordinary offering to an ordinary human being. Mourning creates a personality and collective out of death. The celebration of Moharram is the greatest metaphor for mourning. Mourning comes as Moharram. It comes as a procession. It comes as a possession. It is mourning that defies death and the authorities. It defies the rules of the God of death. One who is living wants to die. One who is dead asks to make a comeback. What else! It is about feeling the other's pain and wound on our own body.

The Tajik government did not exactly want to ban mourning itself, but the excessive emotion that can be radicalized as politics during the death procession. The Tajik authorities said that the law was enacted to stop Islamic radicalization. I am not going into the specific cultural politics of Tajikistan, but we can underline that the act and potential attached to mourning can be seen to lead to radicalization. This fear was palpable in Kashmir. It is believed that after the death and mourning procession of

2021), 27.

the young militant, Burhan Wani, hundreds of youth joined the movement. Similarly, there are instances where after participating in the mourning procession, students from universities joined the various movements in India. Instead of creating fear among the youth, mourning persuaded them in extraordinary ways.

Mourning can be a spectacular act, but it can also be persuasive. The authorities, in general, are afraid of this powerful act of mourning. Anna Kurian observes that 'observing such public commemoration is true of deaths that might cause "social unrest".[16] The funeral of rape victims is usually held secretively. After the brutal rape cases in Delhi and Hathras in Uttar Pradesh, the funerals were held amid tight security. The cremation of the Hathras victim was conducted in the dead of night, and her family was denied the right to perform her funeral rites.

Amidst the pandemic, the Indian state not only tried to remove the shrouds from the dead bodies; they also tried to ban mourning and processions. In a gut-wrenching case in the Indian state of Uttar Pradesh, the authorities did not allow the mother to see the dead body of a rape-victim daughter who was brutally raped and killed by upper-caste men. Similar situations had unfolded during the mass deaths of the pandemic when the state did not allow mourning to take place for fear of 'social unrest'. Not to save the soul of the dead but to save their regime.

Mourning is not just about opening up emotions; it is also about slowly coming to terms with immense loss. It helps us to make meaning and provides closure. It helps us to heal from the loss that remains unsurmountable.

Mourning Banned in Hathras

What happens when a funeral procession is banned and grieving itself is perceived to be a threat? One is not allowed to

---

[16] Anna Kurian, 'Why We Should Collectively Mourn the COVID Dead', *The Wire*, 25 May 2021, https://thewire.in/rights/collective-mourning-covid-19-victims-memorial-india

grieve. One is not allowed to touch the dead. One weeps, but not aloud. That is what the authorities decreed in Hathras in 2020. An inconsolable mother just wanted to kiss the forehead of her daughter who died after days in the hospital, battered after being gang-raped by four upper-caste men. The authorities would not allow her. They would not let the vehicle with the young woman's body stop at the family home. Even as her relatives threw themselves in front of the vehicle, it was driven to the cremation ground.

This decision not to allow the family to grieve at the woman's last rites was not a lapse. It conveyed a profound meaning. It was a clear sign of the state's insecurity. A sign that the young woman had achieved martyrdom. An inconvenient martyrdom. Not the kind of martyrdom that could be televised to rally the nation's collective conscience. It was a death the authorities would have rather ignored. Since they were not able to do so, they chose to burn the woman's body in the dead of night.

Grieving and mourning are at the core of what makes us human. It is an act that heals the deepest wounds of humanity. One obvious reason for the hasty cremation was to destroy any evidence of rape and violence, but it is also clear that they were afraid of the power of mourning. The woman's death had already created an uproar among Dalit communities. The authorities feared that her funeral would turn into a political procession.

This is something that the present dispensation has used to benefit itself greatly. It has frequently valorized death and deployed it to cynical effect. Especially in the case of soldiers' deaths, mourning becomes a national ritual. But egalitarian mourning has been a cause for alarm. While the nation's mourning is a spectacle, egalitarian mourning is a moment of void. Amidst the silent tears is an opportunity for a genuine dialogue with the dead — for profound reflection.

Such mourning is filled with the awareness of social wrongs. It is about making the promise that this will not be allowed to happen again. As Judith Butler notes, mourning is a time when we see human relations differently — we identify with those around us, not from a sense of pride but from a sense of vulnerability.[17] Our concerns may be different, but there is a chance that mourning will generate a new sense of solidarity. It is moments of moral and ethical encounter and confrontation that open the opportunity for change to occur. But as Butler says, there is no guarantee that this will happen. Still, we cannot give up hope. Even if only a few realize the potential of such moments, they will pave the way for social transformation.

In Indian caste society, this comes with a serious warning: mourning and vulnerability should not become permanent emotions. Mourning should not become a mode of identification as it is for *rudaalis* — professional mourners in Rajasthan who express grief at upper-caste funerals.

It is believed that upper-caste men should not display their emotions. Grieving undermines their social status and their masculinity. That is why they hire *rudaalis* to mourn their dead. The *rudaalis* rent out their exhibitions of grief the way contract killers are up for hire. This is a sign of how caste kills human emotions. It kills the meaning of life, birth, and death. It kills the sense of grief and celebration. Contacts become contracts where everything, from sin to mourning, can be bought and sold. Still, genuine grief cannot be outsourced; it can only be shared.

While the nation's mourning is a spectacle, egalitarian mourning is empty — a moment of void. It is a moment of genuine dialogue with the dead, face to face, in the eyes, in the silent tears and screams. It is a deep moment of inner reflection. It is about being guilty of social wrongs. It is about owning death. It is about making the promise that we will not let it happen again. There is no doubt that it can be pretentious as well, but not always. Mourning is about deep human bonds. It is about touch; it is about

17   Judith Butler, *Precarious Life: The Powers of Mourning and Violence* (London: Verso, 2006), 43.

consolation. It is about lifting and standing by. It is about crying together. There is no other moment in human life that can offer us this possibility of genuine solidarity. Whatever may be our fate, we should not lose our faith in collective grieving. Nothing else, only true love and true mourning, can create a constitutive moment for transformative politics.

Who knows, people who are mourning now with a sense of guilt may kill the victim again in the name of merit. Yet, we cannot give up hope. One should not leave the high moral-ethical ground — the substance of egalitarian politics. Suppose it happens the other way around. Even if it happens only for a few, even then, we are moving a step towards the annihilation of caste. Once it happens, it will change the nature of the encounter itself, between you and me, between them and us.

Mourning is not the end. It is not only a sign of death and loss. It is also a symbol of living. Indeed, it is more about living. It is more about what is left. What remains? The saree in the drawers, the toys smiling behind the walls, a shirt hanging on a line, the handkerchiefs that a person missed taking with them. The memories that open up in a series of memories, the desire to live that cannot be killed, the dream that could not be fulfilled. The handwritten signatures lying on the table. The last phone call. The hug and touch. The dead remain in stories and songs. They remain in our dreams and in our hopes that cannot be dashed. Amidst the grieving and mourning, there is hope in the land of open graves.

Epilogue

Yet, Not Yet Over

> *I know the world is bruised and bleeding, and though it is important not to ignore its pain, it is also critical to refuse to succumb to its malevolence. Like failure, chaos contains information that can lead to knowledge — even wisdom. Like art.*
>
> — Toni Morrison[1]

'Shall we conclude?' 'Is it the end of everything?' Of rights and freedom of expression? Of life and art? An immobilizing ideology of our time and a section of liberal scholars are talking about the end. In desperation, they are harking back to history. *How things were so good, now it is so bad.* They have suddenly found the golden days in the past. It was the golden age when art was at work without interruption. The production of knowledge did not have interference. The nation was on the move — with jobs, development, and a rising GDP. As it happened with every death, all the scoundrels became suddenly great. It was hard to believe that the architect of the UAPA was talking about human rights and freedom of expression. The person who ushered in neoliberalism was talking against the selling of state-owned companies. The leaders who led riots became saints.

Some think that things are really getting bad, they should pack their bags. They are looking for safe locations. They may secure their tickets in the heavenly cities of the world. Where will the others go?

---

[1] 'No Place for Self-Pity, No Room for Fear', *The Nation*, 23 March 2015.

The narrator is still standing there thinking about the situation.

Authoritarianism hasn't come in a matter of days. It has been building for years. The hatred that we see in the streets has a history. Cities and villages, too, have a genealogy. The development model that you felt so proud of, displaced millions of Adivasis from their homelands. The religion that you felt so proud of, has been running a slave factory. Since you feel the heat, you think this is the end. Your security, your universities, and your freedom of expression were exceptions to the rule. But the problem with authoritarianism is that it doesn't stop. It wants to capture everything. It wants to take everything down. When it was for others, you thought it was insignificant. When it comes to you, you think this is the end.

The narrator is still standing there! Laughing on this end. He knows no one will accept this end. He is not giving a utopian slogan. He is just sharing the pragmatism of life. Life and art don't end this way.

The curtailment of life and freedom expects to find its culmination in closure, in death, mourning, and mayhem. It wants to end the stories. It claims the end of history. It wants to declare the end. But this is what doesn't happen. Hope refuses to die. Every time a body encounters a barricade, it ends up in a new possibility.

The narrator is still standing there smiling on this end. He is showing us a dancing body in a dead sea, the flowers blooming on a dead tree. On the other side, the authorities want to declare the end. The end of history, the end of an era, the end of politics. The narrator assures us: Don't worry. They haven't read enough history. They are new to power. They are new to civilization. When the regime declares the end, the old narrator laughs so loud that the regime gets afraid. When there was the declaration of the end, he was cracking jokes like any other day. The narrator loves the demagogue. He is obsessed with authority. He is a fan of the dictator. The authority tracks every movement of the narrator; the narrator tracks every move of the authority. As a true artist, he loves to attack the authority. The narrator expressed his hidden desire.

'I wish there was an authoritarian regime; I wish there was a dictator.' When the octogenarian playwright and theatre director Habib Tanvir made this statement against the backdrop of the Gujarat riot of 2002, the audience was shocked.[2] There was a murmur around. 'He has gone insane', said one. 'What is this?' asked another. After a long, theatrical pause, Tanvir continued, 'So I can continue my theatre'. In old age, with shaky fingers, he lit a cigar. He slowly reiterated: 'Yes, I want a dictator, so I can continue with my theatre'. 'Theatre will be boring if we didn't have these characters', he added.

It was the earnest hope of the narrator that theatre can fight an authoritarian regime. It can defeat a dictator. It can drag them out with its drum. It also shows how little importance the narrator gives to the authority. The narrator knows that the biggest weapon unleashed by any authoritarian regime is fear. It wants us to live in fear — the fear of numbers, the fear of the majority, the fear that if you do not vote, the nation will fall. But the authority feels afraid if we stop fearing. The point is not to lose hope. The point is not to succumb to the malevolence of power.

The narrator is getting bored of tragedy. The same agonizing stories. He realized that these tragedies were so bad that they didn't give him any cathartic experience. He decided to read Greek comedy. Then he laughed again.

There is a scene of a shouting match between Cleon and the Sausage Seller: Each man strives to show that he is a more shameless and unscrupulous orator than the others. The narrator was too lazy to laugh. He goes slowly: '*Ye log aate jate rahta hai yaar*' (They keep coming and going). With his cigar, the narrator makes an exit, smiling and cracking jokes about the authority.

---

[2] The conversation is based on Habib Tanvir's public talk delivered at Jawaharlal Nehru University, New Delhi, on 1 September 2002. The programme was organized by Barhrup Arts (Theatre) group, Delhi.

We are living in a desperate situation. We have been feeling short of breath. Democracy was never such a blank sheet of paper. It seems that the promises we made all end here. But this is not the end. This is where closure — the end — gets entangled with the opening. Life and art often spring from that closure. The greatest love epics could only become possible in feudal societies. Remember the epic of Heer Ranjha, the play of Romeo and Juliet, and the ballad of Reshma-Chuharmal. Most beautiful poetry and epics are written against the backdrop of curtailment. Should we accept curtailment? Nobody says so. These stories are a simple but remarkable statement on how life and art do not end in curtailment.

After the suppression of the anti-CAA-NRC protests, the authority was emboldened that it would be the end of the minorities' dissents in India. They will be silenced forever. But that didn't happen. As soon as they exited, the farmers filled that space. Women and children were back again. After the authorities passed a law against love (anti-conversion law), more lovers ran away from home, risking their lives. When the government left us at the mercy of Covid-19, we saw a new assembly emerge. Within days, people created a parallel system of governance. Like the beautiful wind, they came against the end.

We are not making an exit. This is not the end. We are only taking a pause. We will meet again at the barricades, in words, for life and freedom. A popular saying goes that the barricade closes streets but opens ways.

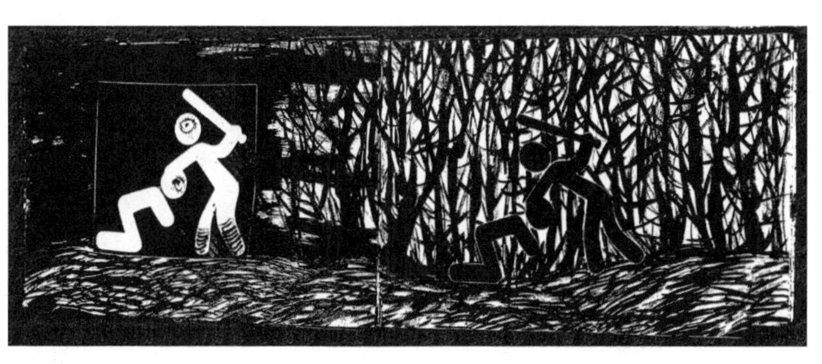

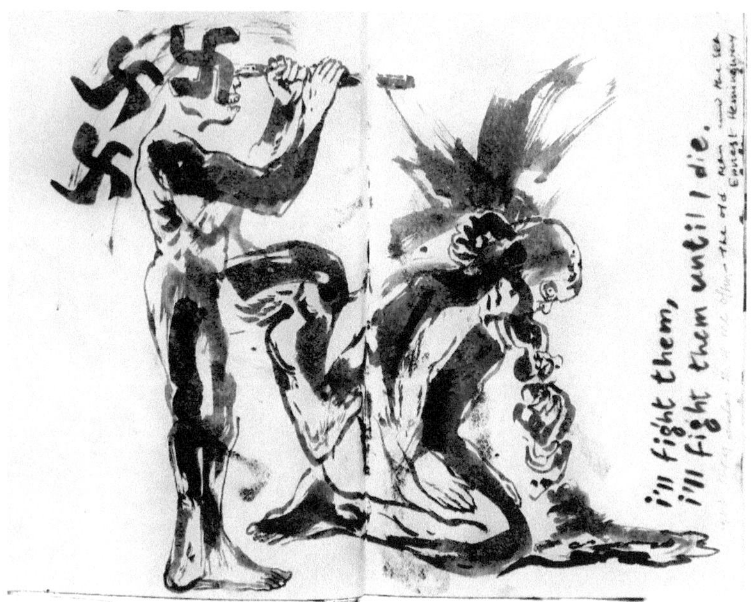

i'll fight them,
i'll fight them until I die.
the old man and the sea
Ernest Hemingway

Acknowledgements

This book of essays was not planned, it came out of the blue. It came out as a response to the emerging socio-political situations. Perhaps it was my association with street theatre that set the stage. I used to write songs and plays for street theatre. In street theatre, one has to respond to situations on an urgent basis. Sometimes, it was a play against communalism, sometimes it was a song against displacement. I express my gratitude to my friends and comrades at various street theatre groups I was associated with — Janrang, Jugnu, and RCF — for this training.

This book has its own journey. In 2018, a right-wing newspaper approached me to write a column. I wrote it, not to be published further, but that made me realise that I could write. That I can tell the stories. That I can connect beyond the academic world. The act of writing that was so intimidating for me suddenly became liberatory when I started writing in my direct voice, in my felt verse. I would like to thank all the platforms which gave me the space to write: Indian Cultural Forum, *Outlook*, Scroll.in, The Quint, The Wire, and others.

Sometimes it may happen that when you are denied a good education, you become Eklavya. You create images of your desired teachers. You imitate them, you practice under their shadows. I invented many such teachers. I follow John Berger to find my perspective; I read Arundhati Roy aloud to find the lyrics. bell hooks is my mother who gives me the meaning and purpose of writing. Gaddar taught me that writing is not about completing a thousand words, it is about giving life to words. That every word is born out of struggle; every word can turn into fire. I thank my school teachers, Manindra Singh, Rajendra Paswan, and S.N. Mishra for igniting my interest in literature. I thank my PhD supervisor, Helen Gilbert, who would fill my drafts with red ink but with immense hope and words of appreciation. I thank H.S. Shivaprakash for inculcating in me a poetic spirit and pushing me to write against the dry and pedantic language of the academic world.

How can I not remember my 'semi-literate' mother who understands the importance of letters but feels that writing is a conspiracy against the world. Behind educating us, her aim was not to make us scholars but to save us from the conspiracy of writing. She made sure that all her children recognize the letter and do not fall into the trap of the written contract. When I write, she thinks I am plotting a conspiracy against people in power. Herself a confrontational person, she thinks that I should not confront those powerful 'big guys'. She is not a great mother who will sacrifice her life for her children. She is not an ideal mother. She is a typical *jhagralu aurat*, who fights for everything, for every inch. She is a social mother, the Mother Courage of Bertolt Brecht, who has to plan everything, from the distribution of food to love and emotions among her children. I thank her for her endless stories, and for teaching me to love and disagree in extreme ways. We rarely agree on any points except one. We both have lots of complaints against this world. Our paths might be different, but we both think that the world has to be changed. She remains my strongest critic: *Go and teach your stupid students who think that after reading a hundred books you have become a pandit (scholar).*

I try my best to keep my critics close. Much love to another woman and critic, to my friend and partner, Sharmistha Mallick, whose love and criticisms keep me passionate and alive. When one tried to understand the world, she helped realise how little we knew about human emotions. How little do we know about the depth of love. How little do we know about the struggle and passion for life. Thanks to the phenomenal woman on stage whose inner mystery keeps surprising me. More than stories, we connect through lyrics and music. I express my gratitude to her family members who have been a huge support.

I express my deep gratitude to my family members who think that I am on some mission to change the world. Lots of love to Anupam, Mangal, Manu, Sandhya, Shubham, and Tanu. I express my gratitude to my sisters, Guddi and Renu Devi, for their support. My younger brother, Dharm Prakash 'Manto', has to do all the thankless jobs of the family. Like always, he has been a constant support, along with Sushma.

I dedicate this book to my love and friendship, to named and unnamed one who all have touched me in this journey. Many times, it feels annoying to have so many friends. They give you a lot of trouble. But then they take all your troubles. So much so that you don't need to worry about your life. You get food, drink, medicines, suggestions, and unsolicited comments. You get criticism that nobody would dare to give you. I express my deep gratitude to all my friends, who stood with me in thick and thin, even though I abandoned them after getting my work done. Perhaps they still believe that my intention was not bad. They still remain my huge support. I want to thank Atul Aditya, Arvind Koshal, Mritunjay K. Yadavendu, Sanjay Kumar, Shashank Yadav, Subrata Das, Sunil Kumar and Varunika Saraf for always having faith in me. I can never compensate for their love and support. I am grateful to Bikramaditya K. Choudhury, Nilanjana Sengupta, Reyazul Haq, Santosh Raut, and Vijay Kumar Yadavendu for their continued support.

The real credit for this work goes to two lovely friends: Nupur Chowdhury and Navaneetha Mokkil. In the pandemic, when the world came to standstill, two 'crazy' women started walking. Allegation goes that I ambushed their group. We ended up walking, chatting, laughing, and forming a formidable Covid-19 club. I started sharing my writings with them. Those write-ups benefited from their comments and ended up becoming full chapters here. I also thank other members of the club who became great friends: Ameet Parameswaran, Meera Gopakumar, Mohinder Singh, Prachinkumar, Shambhavi Prakash, Tobias Toll, and many others.

ACKNOWLEDGEMENTS

I am deeply grateful to Annie Zaidi, Arundhati Roy, Ghazala Jamil, K. Satyanarayana, Nivedita Menon, and Santosh Dass for reading drafts, offering comments, and writing generous endorsements for this book. The book has significantly benefited from the insights of Anusha Kedhar, Navaneetha Mokkil, Pradeep Shinde, Royona Mitra, Udaya Kumar, and others.

It was a pleasure to meet Anupam Roy whose artworks I encountered on the walls but could never meet before. I thank him for sharing his artworks for this book. Thanks also to Aatika Singh, Namita, and Tushar Kanti Saha for helping with the artwork and designing the cover.

I express my sincere gratitude to all my colleagues and office-staffs at the School of Arts and Aesthetics at JNU, New Delhi. They offer you the best. I especially thank Bishnupriya Dutt, Urmimala Sarkar Munsi, and Y.S. Alone for their love and support; and Soumyabrata Choudhury for being a fellow traveller. Lots of love to my students who always teach me more than what I teach them.

I offer my special thanks to the staff at LeftWord Books who saw potential in the manuscript when corporate publishers declined it for its 'volatile language' and unusual style. A positive reply from LeftWord felt like a deep solidarity. This also shows the role of independent publishers in a time of tyranny. Thanks to Vijay Prashad, Sudhanva Deshpande, Winnie Chauhan, and Devi Vijay for taking it forward. I can't thank Devi Vijay and Fuzail Siddiqi enough for their edits and feedback that have enriched the book.

Last but not the least, my deepest love and thanks to my readers and critics, whose comments and feedback on my popular essays and previous book have encouraged me to write this book. Writing has been both a humiliating and humbling experience for me. Your comments make me feel special. This book is for you and countless others who believe in the power of words.